FANTASTIC FEARSOME
Beasts

FANTASTIC
FEARSOME
Beasts

SCARY MONSTERS
OF MYTHS AND LEGENDS

PAULA HAMMOND

SCHOLASTIC

www.scholastic.com

This edition published by Scholastic Inc., 557 Broadway, New York, NY 10012 by arrangement with Amber Books Ltd.

Scholastic Canada Ltd.
Markham, Ontario

Grolier International, Inc.
Makati City, Philippines

1 2 3 4 5 6 7 8 9 10

ISBN: 978-0-545-83120-8

Editorial and design by
Amber Books Ltd
74–77 White Lion Street
London N1 9PF
United Kingdom
www.amberbooks.co.uk

Project Editor: Sarah Uttridge
Design: Keren Harragan

Printed in Shenzhen, China

Picture Credits:
All illustrations by Barry Croucher, Jean-Michel Girard and Terry Pastor / The Art Agency © Amber Books Ltd.

Contents

Introduction

Who doesn't love a spooky story? People have been telling tales guaranteed to give their listeners goosebumps since cave dwellers first lit fires to scare away the shadows. So draw the curtains, dim the lights, and get cozy as we take you on a tour of beastly goings-on from Africa to America, from Greece to Greenland and beyond.

Every culture has its own phantoms, freaks, and fiends. In this book, you'll find forty-four of the most deadly, dire, and downright strange. We have creatures like the undead, flesh-eating Draugr, which was creepy enough to give the Vikings nightmares. Then there is terrifying Tupilaq—said to be made by black magic and fueled by dark desires. We tell the story of the half-dragon, half-woman, Campe, who was so monstrous that the Greek god Cronus used her as his jailer, and of the demonic dog Black Shuck, who appeared as an omen of death and disaster.

Each entry comes fully illustrated and annotated. Additional fact boxes, maps, size guides, and need-to-know information provide you with everything you will need to become an instant expert on some of folklore's most fantastic and fearsome beasts.

But beware before you start reading! The blood suckers, shape shifters, ghosts, ghouls, zombies, and demons in these pages are nothing like the teenage vampires and trendy werewolves that you see in movies. They are dark, dangerous, and deadly.

Of course, we all know that such beasts are the stuff of myths and legends. They come from an age when people believed in magic. They come from a time when the night—without the comfort of electric light—was cold, dark, and full of unexplained sounds and shapes. They come from tales made up by ancient people to explain away events that seemed strange or fearful. Some of them were probably just told to stop naughty children from straying too far from their beds at night!

We hope that you'll enjoy these stories and not get too scared. Just don't worry about that odd shape at the bottom of the bed. It's just an old coat after all, right…?

Ahuizotl

(Ah-wee-zot-el)

TAIL
The Ahuizotl's long tail has a human-looking hand at its end. It uses this to drag its victims to their doom.

HANDS
With five hands, Ahuizotl has no problems grasping and holding its struggling prey in the water.

BODY
The beast's black, slick body is covered in waterproof fur. When wet, the fur clumps together to create spikes.

TEETH
The Ahuizotl drowns its victims and then uses its sharp fangs to pull out their eyes, teeth, and nails.

Night falls, and as people draw closer to their fires to keep out the gathering gloom, a mournful cry breaks the eerie silence. Somewhere close by it sounds as if a lost child is weeping. However, in this Aztec city, people know better than to go out looking for the source of such sounds. Ahuizotl is a legendary beast who likes to drag villagers into the river and drown them. It is said that when he is especially hungry, he cries like a child in the hope that some unsuspecting adult will come looking for the lost baby and end up on his menu!

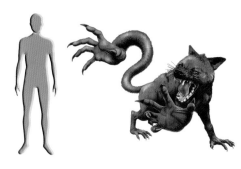

ACTUAL SIZE

▶ IT HAS BEEN A HOT MORNING AND NAHUI HAS WORKED UP A THIRST. Heading toward the river for a drink, he hears a strange rustling and catches a glimpse of something black and shiny. Before he can find out what it is, a doglike figure darts out of the undergrowth. The beast's tail lashes toward him and a cold, wet hand grabs his wrist and pulls him off his feet. Horrified, Nahui struggles frantically against Ahuizotl's strong grip as the fiend drags him toward the edge of the water.

Where in the world?

Ahuizotl comes from Aztec mythology. The Aztecs lived in central Mexico, although the word "Aztec" can be used to describe the inhabitants of Tenochtitlan (modern Mexico City).

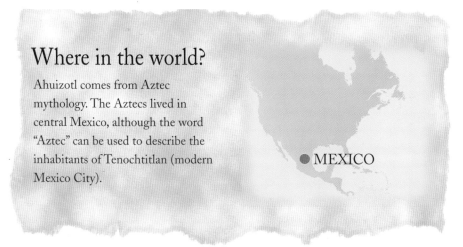

● MEXICO

Did you know?

● Ahuizotl is described in Book XI of *The Florentine Codex*. This was an amazing document written by a friar called Bernardino de Sahagun between 1545 and 1590. Friar Bernardino's *Codex* is one of the most important books about this time.

● Some scientists think that Ahuizotl is based on the real-life giant otter. These animals are very clever hunters who will sometimes feed on the flesh of corpses. They are said to especially like the soft fingertips, lips, and eyes!

● According to Aztec beliefs, anyone who is killed by Ahuizotl, or who dies violently in water, spends their afterlife in the realm of Tlaloc. Tlaloc was the god of rain and water and his home, called Tlalocan, was described as being a paradise of eternal springtime.

● The name Ahuizotl comes from *atl*, meaning "water," *huiz*, meaning "thorn" (for its wet, spiky fur) and *otl*, meaning "like."

Aigamuchab

(Eye-ga-much-ab)

HANDS
With a pair of strong hands, this beast can catch and hold its victims while his teeth do their grisly work.

MOUTH
The beastly Aigamuchab is a man-eater with powerful teeth and jaws that allow him to tear through human flesh!

BODY
Aigamuchab may look like a man but he is a monster. He has a tough, stocky body, designed for the hunt!

FEET
These creepy creatures have one fatal flaw: Their eyes are on the soles of their feet. That means they can't see where they're running.

Lying in wait beneath the baking sand dunes of the Kalahari Desert is one of Africa's most feared creatures. The Aigamuchab may look like a man, but he is as powerful as an ogre—and he has a taste for eating human flesh! This weird beast comes from the legends of the San people, whose stories date back for thousands of years. In fact, the San are one of humankind's oldest ancestors. All modern humans originally came from hunter-gatherer tribes just like the San people. So, who knows, the Aigamuchab may well be one of our oldest nightmares!

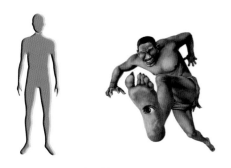

ACTUAL SIZE

► KXARU DIDN'T LIKE WALKING ACROSS THE SAND DUNES TO THE WATERING HOLE. It was there that the fearsome Aigamuchab made his home, and he was always hungry! Luckily, Kxaru's grandmother had told her all about the creature. She knew that there was one easy way to escape from his vicious claws and sharp teeth—run! With eyes on the soles of his feet, he was running blind, so as long as she was speedy and silent she had a good chance of not becoming his next meal.

Where in the world?

Myths about Aigamuchab were born in the area of the Kalahari Desert. This is a massive desert area that stretches out across Angola, Botswana, Namibia, South Africa, Zambia, and Zimbabwe.

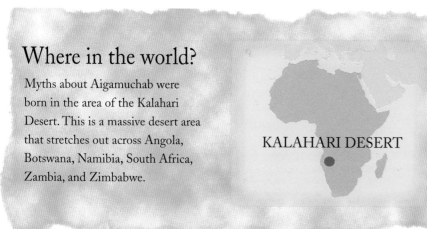

KALAHARI DESERT

Did you know?

• The San people are nomads (wandering people) who make their homes in the Kalahari Desert. Life in the Kalahari can be very tough. In fact, "Kalahari" means "great thirst"!

• Many of the San's myths and legends are recorded in cave paintings, and these can be found throughout southern Africa. Some of these are 3,000 years old.

• On his own, this beast is called Aigamuchab. However, when these creatures hunt in a pack, they are known as Aigamuxa.

• Aigamuchab is just one of many creatures that appear in San legends. They also tell tales about a beast called the Bi-Bloux, which is a man-eating monster with one leg and one arm, who must move around by hopping. Ga-Gorib is another beast, said to live in a deep hole, who fools people into coming too close to the pit's edge.

Aspidochelone

(As-pi-do-ke-lo-nee)

SPIKES
Large spikes cover the turtle's giant carapace (shell). These are usually hidden by the vegetation that grows on top.

MOUTH
This turtle is the size of a whale, with a massive mouth and crushing jaws.

BODY
Aspidochelone is described as looking like a whale, a giant spiny fish, or a gigantic turtle. Whatever shape it takes, though, it is huge!

ARMS
These claws are impressive, but Aspidochelone is unlikely to use them to catch prey. His key weapons are cunning and surprise.

This vast creature is so massive that trees have taken root on its back, and birds have made their homes in their branches. This makes it all the easier for Aspidochelone to lure unsuspecting sailors to their doom! All this great mythical monster has to do is lie perfectly still and wait for a ship to pass by looking for a place to weigh anchor. Then, once it is certain that its prey has taken the bait, it sinks back beneath the waves, dragging the ship and its hapless crew down into the depths where it can devour their lifeless bodies.

ACTUAL SIZE

► DEUCALION LOOKED CAUTIOUSLY AROUND THE ISLAND. His captain had ordered him to go on shore to see what food was to be found and—after weeks at sea—he had been eager to feel solid ground under his feet. However, now that he was ashore he couldn't help feeling uneasy. It was almost as though he was being watched. And just what had caused that sudden quake, which had shaken the small island so much that he had almost fallen over? He felt certain that something wasn't right…

Where in the world?

Aspidochelone is a myth from Ancient Greece. The beast was said to haunt the waters of the Aegean, Ionian, and Mediterranean seas, surrounding the Greek mainland and islands.

GREECE

Did you know?

• Aspidochelone was mentioned in an Ancient Greek bestiary called *The Physiologus*, which was written around the 2nd century AD. A bestiary was a "book of beasts," which was a bit like a modern-day encyclopedia, only it contained both real and legendary animals.

• *The Lord of the Rings* author J.R.R. Tolkien told a story about a giant Aspidochelone in *The Adventures of Tom Bombadil*. He called his beast Fastitocalon and made up this verse to tell its tale: "Look, there is Fastitocalon! An island good to land upon, Although 'tis rather bare … See seagulls sitting there! Beware!"

• In the World of Warcraft online role playing game, the Wandering Isle was a giant turtle named Shen-zin Su.

• In *Tales of the Thousand and One Nights*, Sinbad the Sailor meets an Arabian version of Aspidochelone, which is called a Zaratan.

Aunyaina

(Un-yen-a)

TUSKS
Boarlike tusks are used to tear his victims into chunks. Powerful jaws allow him to eat both flesh and bones.

MOUTH
Can there be anything more terrifying than staring into the mouth of a monster whose favorite snacks are children?

BODY
Aunyaina is large and beastlike—much more like an ogre than a man.

ARMS AND LEGS
This is a beast built for strength and speed. He has large, muscular arms, and powerful legs.

The Tupari people of Brazil have their own version of the tale of "Jack and the Beanstalk," only their giant is much less friendly! Aunyaina is an enormous beast, with tusks like a boar. He feeds on anyone unlucky enough to cross his path. He is especially fond of children, whom he tears apart with his tusks and eats, bones and all! In one version of the story, some children climb a tree to escape from him. Aunyaina is too big to climb up after them through the flimsy branches, so he climbs up a vine instead. A friendly parrot chews through the vine, and the beast crashes to the ground and is killed.

ACTUAL SIZE

▶ IN ANOTHER VERSION OF THE STORY, THE BEAST IS CHASING A MAN THROUGH A FOREST CLEARING. Aunyaina is so close that he can almost reach out and grab him! In desperation, the man grasps a thick vine from the forest floor and throws it up into the sky. To his amazement, it hangs there, like a ladder to the clouds. He frantically climbs up it, with Aunyaina just behind him. The parrot flies to his aid, chewing through the vine and sending the beast crashing down to his death.

Where in the world?

Aunyaina lives in the forest. He haunts the places where the Tupari people make their homes, around the Rio Branco in the state of Rondônia, Brazil.

● BRAZIL

Did you know?

● There are many versions of this popular tale. In one account, when the beast falls from the vine his body splits apart. Lizards burst out of his corpse and scurry away to colonize the land.

● In some versions of the story, while the children are lucky enough to escape being eaten by the hungry beast, they are turned into monkeys and spend the rest of their lives in the treetops.

● Tupari myths include gods, demons, magicians, and monsters. However, the story of Aunyaina has spread beyond Tupari culture. He is a popular character in online role-playing games and has his own entry on godchecker.com!

● When the Tupari people first met outsiders in the early 20th century, they called them Tarüpa. Tarüpa means "bad spirits." This was a reference to the problems that the outsiders brought with them, including terrible diseases.

Az-I-Wu-Gum-Ki-Mukh-Ti

(Az-ee-woo-gum-kee-muk-tee)

HEAD
Az-I-Wu-Gum-Ki-Mukh-Ti is described as looking like a gigantic walrus with the legs, paws, and head of a dog.

TAIL
At the end of the beast's oversized body is a huge fish tail—perfect for lashing out at passers-by.

BODY
As can be seen, Az-I-Wu-Gum-Ki-Mukh-Ti has a powerful and muscular body, which is covered in layers of gleaming black scales.

PAWS
Monstrous doglike paws, complete with claws, and sturdy arms make this beast look even more scary.

There is something truly unsettling about this freakish beast from the frozen North. Az-I-Wu-Gum-Ki-Mukh-Ti is a monster from the legends of Greenland's Inuit people. These people are used to the hardships and dangers of living in one of the world's most difficult regions. Yet, Az-I-Wu-Gum-Ki-Mukh-Ti is spoken about in fearful whispers.

ACTUAL SIZE

Looking like something cobbled together in a mad scientist's lab, Az-I-Wu-Gum-Ki-Mukh-Ti has the head, paws, and legs of a dog, the tail of a fish, and the body of a walrus, covered in black scales. He is built on a gigantic scale and is said to enjoy the taste of human flesh!

▶ THE DAY WAS FRESH AND CLEAR, WITH THAT CHILLY FALL STING that always made Najannguaq feel glad to be alive. Out across the ice, where the seas were still unfrozen, she could see whales jumping and playing. It was a fantastic sight. She was so wrapped up in the thrill of it that she did not see the danger coming. Throwing itself out of the water with a roar that sent shivers down Najannguaq's spine, Az-I-Wu-Gum-Ki-Mukh-Ti attacked. Najannguaq would have to move quickly if she wanted to live!

Where in the world?

Az-I-Wu-Gum-Ki-Mukh-Ti is a creature of water and ice who was believed to live in the chilly Arctic waters around Greenland, Northern Canada, and America.

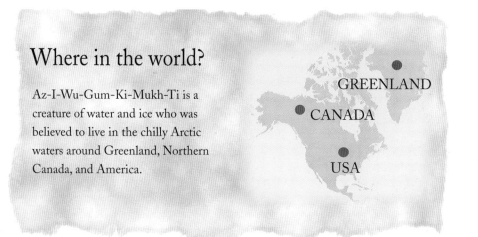

GREENLAND

CANADA

USA

Did you know?

● Az-I-Wu-Gum-Ki-Mukh-Ti may be mythical, but leopard seals have been known to attack people who get too close to the edge of the ice floe. So it is possible that Inuit tales of creatures such as Az-I-Wu-Gum-Ki-Mukh-Ti were made up to try to stop children from wandering too near the sea, where real dangers could lie in wait.

● The Inuit believe that all things have a soul and that, if you treat animals badly, their spirits may come back for revenge. Part of the job of a traditional *angakkuq* (shaman) was to defend the community against real and spiritual threats, like Az-I-Wu-Gum-Ki-Mukh-Ti.

● Inuit tales were passed on by word of mouth for thousands of years before they were ever written down. The tales tell us much about their life, beliefs, and customs, as well as recording their love of a good, creepy fireside story!

Behemoth
(*Be-hee-muth*)

TAIL
The creature's tail is described as looking like a cedar tree. Cedar trees are evergreen and have spiky leaves.

BODY
Behemoth was said to be a combination of many real and mythical animals. He looks part elephant, part crocodile, and part hippo.

SKIN
In his poem "The Seasons," Scottish poet James Thomson describes Behemoth as having armored skin: "behold! in plaited mail, Behemoth rears his head."

SIZE
English poet John Milton said in his poem "Paradise Lost" that Behemoth was the "biggest born of earth." Behemoth means "huge."

The Behemoth is a monster from Jewish and Christian literature. This creature lived in the boiling chaos that existed before creation. It is said that he will return at the end of days to fight with another beast of the void—the Leviathan. No one can agree on what a Behemoth looks like. Some say it resembles an elephant, some a hippo,

ACTUAL SIZE

buffalo, or a crocodile. Others believe that it is a mixture of all the world's mythical beasts. In the ancient Jewish "Book of Enoch", the Behemoth is described as being an unconquerable monster. This would make it the world's most fearsome beast.

▶ "… THE LEVIATHAN AND THE BEHEMOTH … WILL INTERLOCK WITH ONE ANOTHER and engage in combat … with his horns the Behemoth will gore the Leviathan [who] will leap to meet him with his fins …. Their Creator will approach them with his mighty sword [and kill them both] … from the beautiful skin of the Leviathan, God will construct canopies to shelter the righteous, who will eat the … Behemoth and the Leviathan amid great joy and merriment…." (From *Artscroll prayer-book*, page 725.)

Where in the world?

Behemoth was said to live in an invisible desert called Dundayin, east of the Garden of Eden. British Egyptologist Dr. David Rohl thinks that Eden was in modern-day Iran.

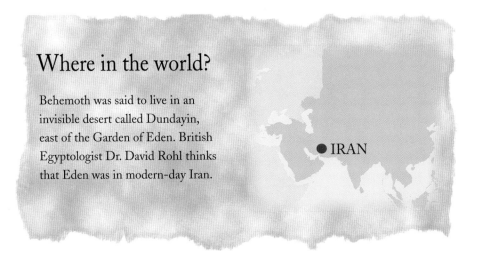

● IRAN

Did you know?

• According to the "Book of Enoch," Behemoth is the primordial (first) beast of the land. Leviathan is his counterpart in the sea, while Ziz rules the air. However, in Jewish and Christian traditions God was so powerful that he treated Behemoth like a pet and led it around on a leash attached to a ring through its nose!

• Behemoth was the name chosen by a hugely successful Polish heavy metal band from Gdansk. The band was formed in 1991.

• The Canadian Maneater Series of made-for-TV movies specializes in stories about "natural horrors." *Behemoth* was made in 2011 and was the 23rd film in the series, which also includes swamp devils, yetis, werewolves, and hellhounds.

• In a series of steampunk books by American science fiction author Scott Westerfeld, Behemoth is the name of a fabulous "fabricated animal" that can swallow battleships whole.

Bhainsasura

(Bane-sa-sure-a)

HORNS
A pair of huge horns curve out toward the back of the beast's head. The horns grow horizontally rather than vertically.

HEAD
Bhainsasura looks like a grotesque overgrown bull. He has a flat forehead, large eyes, and a long, wide muzzle.

BODY
Like a genuine water buffalo, Bhainsasura has a heavy body and stocky build, with a short torso and large belly.

LEGS
Unlike real water buffalos, Bhainsasura walks upright. A pair of large feet and muscular legs add to the beast's impressive physique.

In the villages of Northern India, the everyday tasks of growing food, fishing, and collecting fresh water must be done with extra care, because the fields and lakes are said to be haunted by a spirit who appears in the form of a huge water buffalo. Bhainsasura is like a demon mobster who tramples crops and drowns fishermen unless he is paid "protection money." To protect their harvest, farmers must slaughter pigs and spread the blood on their fields to keep the monster away. Anyone wanting to fish must make an offering of chickens, goats, and eggs to keep this bad-tempered beast satisfied.

ACTUAL SIZE

▶ THE LITTLE BOAT BOBBED UNEVENLY IN THE WATER AS THE GIGANTIC BEAST WADED CLOSER. The men who had come to make the offering glanced at each other in nervous silence. Bhainsasura may have had the familiar look and smell of a water buffalo, but this was no docile domestic animal. Towering above them, Bhainsasura's eyes gleamed with a cruel and wicked intelligence. If he was pleased with their offering, then all would be well. If not, then they would never see their wives and children again.

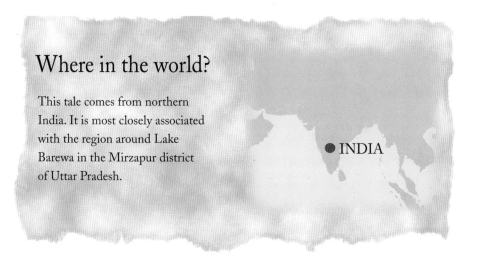

Where in the world?

This tale comes from northern India. It is most closely associated with the region around Lake Barewa in the Mirzapur district of Uttar Pradesh.

● INDIA

Did you know?

● Bhainsasura isn't the only beast that is said to inhabit Lake Barewa. In fact, this famous watering hole has two more demon spirits, known as Nag and Nagin. Nāgas are nature spirits and the protectors of springs, wells, and rivers. In some stories, Nag and Nagin appear in the form of male and female water serpents.

● In many myths, water acts as a doorway between the real world and the world of the supernatural. The water demons who live in these watery realms are said to have treasure troves hidden beneath the waves, with which they tempt greedy humans.

● According to folklore, another Mirzapur river, the Karsa, is just as dangerous as Lake Barewa. It is said that when anyone attempts to drink from the river, the waters bubble up and the resident demon, "with matted hair," sweeps them away.

Bisclavret

(*Bis-clav-ray*)

HEAD
The werewolf has the best of both worlds—the hearing and sense of smell of a skilled hunter, coupled with the intelligence of a human.

TAIL
Although most legends say that werewolves look just like real wolves, they do not have a tail.

LEGS
Werewolves are fast, powerful, and agile beasts. When running on all fours they can easily exhaust their prey.

SKIN
It is said that if you cut the skin of a werewolf in human form, you will see the fur beneath!

Who doesn't love a good werewolf story? One of the earliest tales about these bloodthirsty beasts comes from 12th-century France, but it is man—or rather woman—who is the villain of the piece. Bisclavret is a baron who mysteriously vanishes during every full moon. Eventually he confesses to his wife that he is a werewolf. He asks her to keep his clothes safe, as he needs them to return to his human form. The wife is terrified and hides the clothes, so Bisclavret is trapped in his wolf form. She marries again, but the wolf Bisclavret is so noble that he attracts the attention of the king, who quickly learns the truth.

ACTUAL SIZE

▶ MARIE DE FRANCE WAS A POET WHO WAS PROBABLY BORN IN BRITTANY but worked in England at a time when King Henry II (1133–1189) ruled both regions. She is famous for writing poems that had a huge impact on English literature. We know very little about her life, but it is tempting to imagine her, working crouched over a manuscript, with a flickering candle casting ominous shadows across the room. Perhaps she even stopped writing occasionally to listen to the wolves howling outside?

Where in the world?

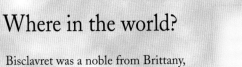

Bisclavret was a noble from Brittany, which is in northwestern France. When the tale was written, Brittany was part of the Angevin Empire.

● FRANCE

Did you know?

● In Marie's tale, Bisclavret, when still trapped in his wolf's body, confronts his wife and bites her nose off!

● A similar story about a werewolf who is betrayed by his wife is told in the tale of Sir Marrok from Sir Thomas Mallory's *Morte d'Arthur*. This was probably based on either the original Breton folk tale or Marie's popular retelling.

● Werewolves and skin walkers are common elements in folk tales. One of the earliest werewolf stories appears in the *Satyricon* by Gaius Petronius Arbiter, who lived at the time of the Roman Emperor Nero (27–66 AD). In it, a character called Niceros says: "[I was looking] for my buddy … I see he'd stripped and piled his clothes by the roadside... and then, just like that, he turns into a wolf!"

Black Shuck
(*Blak shuk*)

EYE
Depending on the storyteller, Black Shuck either has flaming red eyes the size of saucers, or a single eye.

FUR
Shaggy black fur is this beast's most distinguishing feature. The word "Shuck" is said to mean either "shaggy" or "demon."

HEAD
In some accounts, Black Shuck has no head, appearing like some terrible specter out of a Victorian ghost story.

SIZE
Shuck is most often said to be the shape and build of a very large dog—sometimes as big as a horse.

Some tales tell of Black Shuck arriving wrapped in mist, with his one eye blazing. Some tell of the demonic dog materializing in dark graveyards, bringing death to anyone who sees him. Others tell of this fearsome beast being accompanied by a whole pack of ghostly dogs and hunters riding monstrous goats! Stories of Black Shuck have been recorded in eastern England since the 10th century. In one account, Black Shuck is described prowling along dark lanes and fields, but although "his howling makes the hearer's blood run cold, his footfalls make no sound."

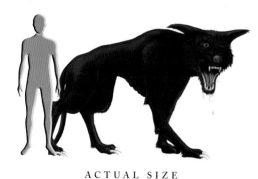

ACTUAL SIZE

▶ ON AUGUST 4, 1577, IN HOLY TRINITY CHURCH, BLYTHBURGH, ENGLAND, a gigantic black dog burst through the doors of the church accompanied by a bolt of lightning. Moving with unholy speed, Black Shuck ran down the aisle, killing two parishioners before bringing the church steeple thundering down through the roof. It is said that, even today, if you visit the church, you can see the scorch marks left on the door by the claws of this demonic hound.

Where in the world?

Tales of ghostly and demonic black dogs crop up all over the British Isles. Black Shuck is especially associated with the counties of East Anglia, Suffolk, and Essex.

EAST ANGLIA

Did you know?

• Later on August 4, twelve miles (19 km) from Blythburgh, Reverend Abraham Flemming recorded that "the likeness of a giant dog" burst into St. Mary's Church, Bungay. In an account called *A Straunge and Terrible Wunder*, he wrote that the dog ran down the aisle of the church "with great swiftnesse." Two people were slaughtered as they knelt to pray. The body of one was left shriveled "like a drawn purse."

• Shuck's attack on Holy Trinity Church is recalled in a ghoulish rhyme from the period: "All down the church in the midst of fire, the hellish monster flew, and, passing onward to the quire, he many people slew."

• In May 2014 archaeologists working on a dig at Leiston Abbey in Suffolk found the skeleton of a seven-foot-long (2.1 m) dog. The abbey's remains are close to Blythburgh and Bungay.

Bruxsa

(Bro-sha)

SHAPE SHIFTING
As a shape shifter, Bruxsa is often linked with legends of the Lobishomen —the name given to werewolves in Portugal.

TEETH
Like all vampires, Bruxsa has a set of sharp canine teeth that she uses to pierce the skin of her victims.

BODY
Bruxsa is not an animated corpse, like many vampires. By day she looks like an ordinary, but very beautiful, woman.

NAME
Bruxsa is the female form of this nighttime terror. Bruxso is the name for the male version of the vampire.

If you think you know all about vampires … then think again! By day the Portuguese Bruxsa looks like an ordinary woman. But by night, she and her evil sisters gather at the crossroads to recite the rituals that transform them into vampires. These dark beauties prey on lost travelers, and have a particular taste for the blood of children. Although sunlight and holy water have little effect on this vampire, Bruxsa, like many magical creatures, is said to be afraid of steel and iron. Mothers would often hammer a nail into the floor or put an amulet under their child's pillow at night to ensure that Bruxsa stayed well away from them!

ACTUAL SIZE

▶ IT WAS A WILD NIGHT AND ALEXANDRE FELT LUCKY TO BE SAFE IN BED. Grandma had been telling him tales of local legends. He didn't believe in vampires and witches, of course. That was just kid's stuff. But as the wind battered the creaking old house, he wished she had chosen some other bedtime stories to tell. Perhaps if he just kept his eyes tight shut, then he'd drift off to sleep and not be bothered by that odd tap-tap-tapping on the window…

Where in the world?

Bruxsa is believed to come from pre-Christian Portuguese legends. When Roman Catholicism spread to Western Europe, Bruxsa was reimagined as a servant of the Devil.

● PORTUGAL

Did you know?

● Eastern European vampires may turn into wolves and bats, but Bruxsa can transform herself into a duck, rat, goose, dove, or even an ant!

● Although Bruxsa is almost impossible to kill, the mother of a child murdered by one of these bloodthirsty fiends does have a unique way of getting revenge. If she boils her child's clothes while stabbing them with a steel pin or cutting them with a pair of steel scissors, then Bruxsa will feel every stab and every cut and will be forced to beg for mercy.

● Bruxsa is a fiend on a schedule! The spell that turns the witch into a vampire must be carried out on Tuesdays or Fridays—both thought of as days of "ill-omen" in Portugal. Her powers were strictly limited to the hours between midnight and 2am.

Campe
(*Cam-pa*)

CLAWS
Campe's long claws are described as "like a crook-talon sickle." A sickle is type of tool with a semicircular blade.

HEAD
Part woman, part dragon, part scorpion, with writhing, poison-spitting serpents for hair, Campe makes a terrifying sight.

TAIL
Over her shoulders rises a monstrous scorpion's tail. It is coiled and poised ready to strike with its deadly sting.

BODY
Campe is sometimes called a sea serpent or a Kētos (a giant fish or whale). Her body is covered with scales.

Campe is a misshapen monstrosity from Greek mythology. The half-dragon version that we see in TV programs and movies, with a woman's upper body and a scorpion's tail, is a shadow of her true self. According to the ancient Greek author Nonnus, she had: "A thousand snakes wrapped round her viperish feet, spitting poison," while "round her neck flowered 50 various heads of wild beasts." Instead of hair she had "spitting serpents" and "from her eyelids a flickering flame belched out far-traveling sparks." Among her powers, she was able to stir up storms and create gales.

ACTUAL SIZE

► AS FAR BELOW HADES AS THE SKY IS ABOVE THE EARTH lies the deep abyss that the great god Cronus uses as his place of torment and punishment. There, three one-eyed giants, the Cyclopes, sit in sullen silence. The brothers, called Arges, Brontes, and Steropes, are strong and skillful. They can craft magical weapons that can kill the gods themselves. Fearing their power, Cronus imprisoned the Cyclopes, setting the monstrous demon Campe as their guard. The prison remained unbreached until Zeus killed Campe and freed her prisoners.

Where in the world?

Ancient Greeks believed that their souls went to Hades after death. Tartarus, which lies far below Hades, was where those souls were judged and punished.

● GREECE

Did you know?

• The name Campe, or Kampê, comes from the Greek meaning crooked or twisting.

• The Cyclopes—Arges, Brontes, and Steropes—created Poseidon's trident, Artemis's bow, the helmet that was given to Perseus to help him kill Medusa, and Zeus's bolts. The brothers each added one element to Zeus's weapons. These additions reflect the meaning of their given names. Arges added brightness, Brontes added thunder, and Steropes added lightning.

• Cronus was the leader of the Titans. He gained power by overthrowing his father, Uranus. Cronus was, in turn, overthrown by his son, Zeus, who became king of the Olympians.

• The 5th-century Greek writer Hesychius of Alexandria described Campe in his "Alphabetical Collection of All Words" as a giant fish, whale, or sea monster like a Kētos (see the entry for Cetus on the next page).

Cetus

(See-tus)

SIZE
Cetus is the Romanized version of the Greek Kētos. Cetus means "large sea animal." In biology, whales are known as cetaceans.

MOUTH
This giant gaping mouth, lined with daggerlike teeth, is easily big enough to swallow the helpless Andromeda whole.

TAIL
Just one flick from this enormous fishy tail could create a deadly whirlpool or whip up tsunami-sized waves.

BODY
Whether inspired by a whale, a giant eel, or an oversized fish, Cetus is an awe-inspiring beast of incredible size and strength.

Cassiopeia had always been proud of her daughter, Andromeda, but the queen's boastful nature had brought disaster to the Ethiopian kingdom. Cassiopeia had declared that Andromeda was more lovely than the Nereids—the daughters of the sea god Poseidon. In a fit of fury, the spiteful god lashed the kingdom's shores

ACTUAL SIZE

with storms, and flooded its cities, wrecking fishing boats and destroying homes. In desperation, the queen sought the advice of a wise woman, who said that Poseidon could only be calmed if Andromeda were sacrificed to Cetus.

► NOTHING COULD HAVE PREPARED ANDROMEDA for the sight of the monstrous beast rising out of the water before her. Although the princess was tied to the rock, she instinctively shrank back as the creature lunged toward her with a blood-curdling roar. As she did so, out of the corner of her eye she saw a remarkable sight. A young man, holding a blood-stained bag, was hovering in the air supported by the flapping wings on the heels of his sandals!

Where in the world?

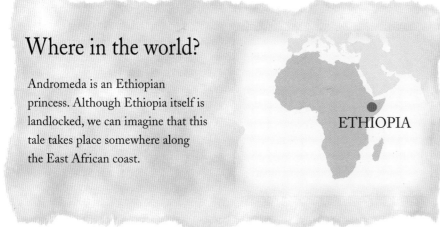

Andromeda is an Ethiopian princess. Although Ethiopia itself is landlocked, we can imagine that this tale takes place somewhere along the East African coast.

ETHIOPIA

Did you know?

• The hero Perseus rescues Andromeda using the severed head of the Gorgon, Medusa, to turn the terrifying Cetus to stone. Medusa was one of three Gorgons, and the only one who could be killed. A version of this tale is retold in the 1981 film *Clash of the Titans*.

• After defeating Medusa, Perseus flies away on his winged sandals. At this point in the story, he seems to get a little power-crazed. On the way, he gets into an argument with Atlas, the Titan whose duty it is to hold up the sky, and ends up turning him into stone.

• Later in the story, Perseus discovers that Andromeda is engaged to her uncle, Phineus. So he turns Phineus to stone, too! Then, once he arrives back home, he turns his uncle, King Polydectes, to stone as well!

Cheeroonear

(Cheer-oon-ee-ar)

TEETH
This monster has doglike teeth but this is certainly no friendly household hound!

ARMS
Although he is humanoid in appearance, Cheeroonear's arms are so long that they drag on the ground as he walks.

BELLY
Cheeroonear's belly is folded, allowing him to suck down lakes in one sitting, and eat children whole.

BODY
Tall and lithe, Cheeroonear is a monster whose body is designed to cope with the baking sands of Australia's great deserts.

"I will return in the morning and command my dogs to kill the men, women, youths, and maidens. But the children, I will save so that I may have my wife prepare me an infant when I wish to eat." It was only an hour since Cheeroonear had delivered this chilling threat. The beast had a seemingly endless appetite and hunted and killed humans

ACTUAL SIZE

for food, accompanied by his wife and pack of six huge dogs. Now the people had to decide what to do. One thing was certain. Although every instinct told them to run away, they were not prepared to let the old and sick fall behind to fill this monster's empty belly…

▶ THE ELDER STOOD IN THE CIRCLE, his eyes blazing with fierce determination. "Cheeroonear will not drive us from our homes," he cried. "He will not take our wives and our children. This morning, we will make a stand. It will be Cheeroonear who will end up as dust and bones, not us!" The men crouched, weapons in hand, tense and alert. The old man's words had put fire in their bellies. Now it was up to them to turn his words into actions!

Where in the world?

Cheeroonear is believed to be a beast from the rich culture of Australia's Spinifex people. This tribe traditionally lived in the Great Australian Desert.

● AUSTRALIA

Did you know?

● In the myths of Australia's first (Aboriginal) people, the Winjarning Brothers were heroes who spent their lives helping those in need. When Cheeroonear made his fearful threat, the Elders of the tribe sent for the Brothers to help them plan their attack on the beast. In other tales, the Winjarnings were called upon to dispose of different monsters, including a race of humans with batlike wings that stretched between their elongated fingers and thumbs.

● People have lived in Australia for at least 75,000 years. They migrated (traveled) from Southeast Asia to Indonesia, until they settled on the island continent. Until the early 1800s, when Europeans began to arrive in Australia, the lives of the Aboriginals had remained untouched by outside influences.

● Many Aboriginal myths have now been written down, but the original stories changed depending on who told them, when, and why.

Cherufe

(*Chair-oof*)

IMAGE
In some accounts Cherufe is described as a dragon. In others, he is a gigantic man with reptilian skin.

BODY
Cherufe lives in the heart of a volcano and his body is created from the same bubbling mass of fiery, liquid rock.

MOUTH
Cherufe is a monster who eats human flesh, especially the flesh of young girls, who are sacrificed to him.

POWER
Cherufe represents the power of Mother Earth, as people used his legend to explain the reason behind earthquakes and volcanic eruptions.

In the bowels of Chile's deepest volcano lives a monster made of flaming magma. This fiendish creation delights in death and destruction, causing volcanoes, earthquakes, and meteorites wherever he treads. There is only one way to calm Cherufe—by throwing a sacrificial victim into his home. Like many beasts, Cherufe has a special liking for young girls, who must be sent alive into the raging lava. It is said that Cherufe has a particularly ghoulish sense of humor. Once he has eaten his fill, he will toss his victim's head down the mountain, much to the distress of her friends and family waiting below.

ACTUAL SIZE

▶ SAYEN HAD NEVER FELT SO AFRAID. The heat from the volcano was almost unbearable. Her mouth was dry and her heart was pounding so hard that it felt as if it would jump out of her chest. The old woman, who was the village shaman, had told her that the volcano was almost ready to erupt. If Cherufe wasn't satisfied, then he would send fire and rock raining down on everyone she loved. She knew that her sacrifice would save them all, but she still felt afraid.

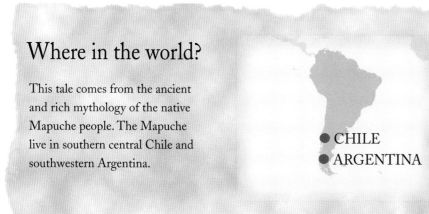

Where in the world?

This tale comes from the ancient and rich mythology of the native Mapuche people. The Mapuche live in southern central Chile and southwestern Argentina.

● CHILE
● ARGENTINA

Did you know?

● According to legend, to protect his people from the ravages of Cherufe, the sun god sent his two warrior daughters to guard the beast. With them they brought a pair of magical swords, which had the power to freeze the creature solid. Unfortunately, he often escaped from their confines to do mischief!

● It is not surprising that the Mapuche have legends about a magma beast. Chile has around 2,000 active and inactive volcanoes along the Andes. Many of its offshore islands were created by volcanic activity.

● The Chonchon is another mythological beast from Mapuche folk tales. This terror is a bird in the shape of a human head, with feathers, talons, and huge ears instead of wings. Chonchon are created by Mapuche wizards who use a special magical lotion that allows them to detach their heads from their bodies!

Draugr

(Drow-gar)

SKIN
The skin of the Draugr was said to be either the color of "blue-death" or as pale as a corpse.

BODY
The Draugr's rotting body can turn into smoke, allowing the corpse to rise from its grave through solid rock.

FEET
To stop a corpse from turning into a Draugr, its toes were tied together or needles were driven into its feet.

SIZE
Draugr are skilled magic users and can change their size and shape. Some Draugr can be as large as an ox.

People have always had a fear of the undead, and when folk tales are full of scary creatures like zombies, revenants, and lichs, is it any wonder? The Draugr of Viking legend is a rotting body reanimated by the evil will of the deceased. Capable of crushing a man to death, this bloated and stinking corpse is supernaturally strong, and able to change

ACTUAL SIZE

his shape and size at will. Although he spends much of his time jealously guarding his tomb from robbers, the Draugr can enter your dreams and drive you mad. He also has an insatiable appetite, as related in the tale of Aran and Asmund from the 15th century *Gautrek's Saga*.

▶ WHEN ARAN DIED, ASMUND VOWED HE WOULD SIT IN MOURNING with the body of his friend for three days. On the first day, Asmund brought his possessions into the barrow, including his hunting hawk, hound, and horse. That night, Aran rose from the dead and ate the hawk and the hound, leaving not a single bone behind. On the second night, Aran rose up again, and devoured Asmund's horse. On the third night, Aran lunged toward his friend, tearing Asmund's ears off in his eagerness to eat!

Where in the world?

Tales of Draugrs come from Viking legend. Historically, the Vikings were seafaring people who came from Scandinavian northern Europe: Denmark, Norway, and Sweden.

SCANDINAVIA

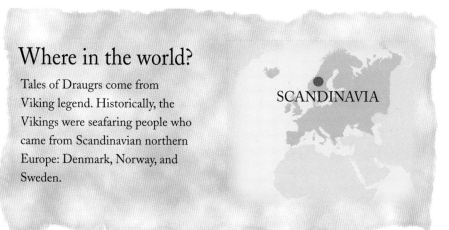

Did you know?

• There were many ways to stop a corpse from rising again. One method, which originated in Denmark, was to use a corpse door. This was a special door, which looked like an oven, built in the home. After a death, the coffin of the departed would be pushed through the corpse door, which was then bricked back up again to prevent a Draugr from returning through it, as spirits were bound to use the same door to leave and enter a home.

• If the corpse was to be interred in a barrow, then the body was carried to the tomb, feet-first, with friends and family gathered close around, so that the corpse could not see where it was going. The body would be moved at least three times before a final resting place was chosen, to confuse any evil spirit.

Each Tened

(Eech ten-ed)

SKIN
Some stories suggest that the horse's skin is sticky, so that the rider is literally glued to its back.

LEGS
Each Tened loves to terrify his rider by making death-defying jumps over fences and hedges, and speeding across the countryside.

HEAD
With a demonic snarl, Each Tened seems to mock those that he traps into riding on his fiery back.

BODY
Each Tened looks like an ordinary horse, until someone tries to mount him. Then, the nature of the beast is revealed!

Not all fearsome beasts bring death and destruction. In Irish folk tales, Each Tened is a demonic fire-horse who carries away and punishes evil-doers. At first glance, the horse looks ordinary enough. Once a rider sits on its back, though, the beast shows its true colors. Its body bursts into flames as it gallops off at break-neck speed. The rider is now locked in a cycle of endless torment, unable to ever dismount, with his flesh continually scalded by the hellish flames. In *The Voyages of the Sons of O'Corra*, three bandits repent their sins and head off on a journey of pilgrimage and discovery, encountering the dreaded Each Tened along the way…

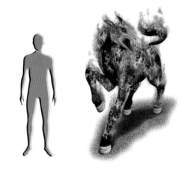

ACTUAL SIZE

▶ "Soon after leaving … [the travelers] saw a horseman of vast size riding on the sea … the horse he rode was made of fire, flaming red … and as he rode … he yelled aloud with fear and pain…. They asked him why he was thus tormented and he answered: 'I am he who stole my brother's horse; and after I had gotten him I rode him every Sunday. For this I am now undergoing my punishment.'" (From *Old Celtic Romances*, translated by P.W. Joyce.)

Where in the world?

The complex cycle of folk tales that make up much of Irish mythology draws on native legends and tales from neighboring Celtic cultures.

● IRELAND

Did you know?

• *The Voyages of the Sons of O'Corra* is a type of tale called an *immram*. In such stories, the hero travels by sea, often to the legendary islands known as the Otherworld, which lie west of Ireland.

• The Highlands of Scotland have a supernatural horse whose element is water rather than fire. Known as Each Uisge (meaning "water horse"), this shape shifter can disguise itself as a horse, a man, or a bird. When Each Uisge is in horse form, he will wait until a traveler mounts him and attempts to ride across water. Then the spirit turns ugly. Dragging its rider into the deepest part of the river, Each Uisge drowns the hapless human and devours him, leaving only the liver behind.

• Dobhar-Chú (water hound) is another monster from Irish myth. This gigantic half-dog, half-otter has been sighted several times since 1684.

Eloko

(Ee-lock-o)

HEAD
Eloko has no hair. Instead, grass grows on his head and over his body, providing camouflage and protection from the elements.

MOUTH
The huge mouth can be flipped open so wide that Eloko is able to swallow a human body whole!

BELLS
Eloko carries little bells which can cast spells on passers-by.

CLOTHES
Eloko dresses himself in leaves, which he gathers from the floor of the rainforest.

Deep in the lush, dark rainforests of the Congo Basin lives a race of diabolical dwarves with a taste for human meat. Eloko is said to be a spirit who has come back to the human world with a grudge to settle. At best, this curious little creature is mean-spirited and jealous. It keeps the ripest forest fruits and tastiest game animals for itself. At worst, it is deadly! Eloko uses bells to cast spells on those who wander too deep into its territory. Its magic is so powerful that once you are under the Eloko's influence, you'll happily stand by while it eats the flesh off your bones.

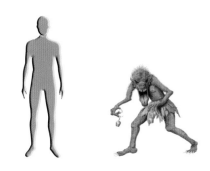

ACTUAL SIZE

► MAYIFA STOOD BESIDE THE DOOR, GRIPPED WITH TERROR. If she put her ear to the wood, she could hear the tinkle of little bells and the shuffle of little feet beyond the threshold. "Hurry, hurry," the bells seemed to say. "Open up and let us in." She knew that she shouldn't. She knew exactly what waited on the other side of the door. Yet, as the bells played their strange tune, she found it harder and harder to resist…

Where in the world?

Eloko inhabits the rainforest of the Congo Basin, although tales of this killer dwarf are told by Bantu-speaking peoples throughout the Congo.

● CONGO BASIN

Did you know?

● Africa is home to 1.1 billion people, and every nation has its own distinct language, culture, and traditions. Tales of the Eloko come from the Bantu language, which is spoken in West and Central Africa.

● Such a huge continent has its share of fearsome beasts, although some seem oddly familiar. For instance, the Kongamato, which is described in tales throughout the Congo, Zaire, and Angola, is described as a flying reptile similar to a Pterosaur. Could it be possible that some remnant of our prehistoric past survives in the huge Congo Basin? Some people think so.

● Although finding a living Pterosaur is unlikely, one legendary beast, known as the Bondo ape, was recently discovered to be a real species of large chimpanzee. This is now known as the Bili ape for the Bili Forest in the Congo where the ape makes its home.

Ethiopian Bull

(Ee-thee-o-pee-an Bull)

HORNS
This bull can move its horns as easily as its ears. When fighting, it makes them stand upright, like daggers.

COLOR
Ancient Greek sources describe this beast as red, although modern writers compare it to the dark brown or black of the buffalo.

SKIN
The bull's bristles can be raised, allowing it to shrug off missiles. Its skin is as tough as iron.

SIZE
Described as twice the size of a normal bull, the Ethiopian bull is a fast, intelligent, and formidable animal.

"It seems," wrote the Roman author Claudius Aelianus in the 2nd century AD, "that these Ethiopian Bulls, which they call flesh-eaters are the most savage of animals.... No spear, no arrow can wound [it] … and it attacks herds of horses and also … [domestic] animals. Accordingly, herdsmen who wish to protect their flocks dig deep concealed ditches and by these means ambush the bulls…. Among the Cave-Dwellers, this is judged to be the king of beasts, and rightly so, for it possesses the courage of a lion, the speed of a horse, the strength of a bull, and is stronger than iron."

ACTUAL SIZE

▶ ETEFU GAZED DOWN INTO THE PIT IN AMAZEMENT. For weeks, something had been savaging his cattle and scaring his dogs. In frustration, he had consulted one of the elders, who had advised him to dig a huge pit … and wait. Etefu had asked what he was waiting for, but the old man had only smiled and said mysteriously, "You will see." Etefu had expected a rogue elephant or maybe a family of wolves, but this beast was the stuff of legend!

Where in the world?

The Federal Democratic Republic of Ethiopia is a country located on the Horn of Africa. When early humans first left Africa, they started their journey from Ethiopia.

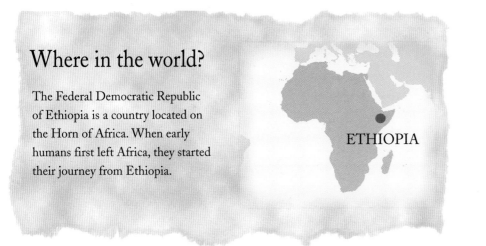

ETHIOPIA

Did you know?

• Folk history, legends, and storytelling are hugely important in Ethiopia. It is believed that many stories date back hundreds of years. Modern retellings of popular tales include cars and TV sets!

• According to accounts by Ancient Greek travelers, little was known about continental Africa. In his *Histories*, which were written in about 444 BC, Herodotus says that Aethiopia was the name given to all of the inhabited land south of Egypt. Aethiopia was, the Ancients believed, a land of gold and ivory where the men were "handsomer, and longer lived than anywhere else."

• The Crocotta is another of Ethiopia's strange mythical beasts. This cunning creature is a combination of a dog and a lion. It imitates human speech to lure unsuspecting victims to their deaths!

• The legendary Sphinx was said to live in the mountains of Ethiopia.

Fjalar & Galar

(*Fee-ar-lar and Gar-lar*)

MIND
The *Prose Edda* says that dwarves are the maggots who feasted on the flesh of Ymir. They therefore have the wisdom of the gods.

MALE OR FEMALE
In legends, dwarves are almost always males with long beards. When female dwarves appear they are temptresses and seducers!

BODY
In the *Poetic Edda*, dwarves are said to be made from the blood and leg bones of the giant Ymir.

SIZE
The earliest Norse tales make no mention of their size. Only later are dwarves referred to as being short and ugly.

One loathsome creature is bad, but two are trouble! Fjalar and Galar are a pair of deadly dwarves from Norse mythology. They appear in an epic collection of Scandinavian myths written by Snorri Sturluson (1179–1241). In one tale, the evil duo lure Kvasir to their cave and murder him. Kvasir was created from the union of the Vanir and the Aesir, two rival groups of gods. The story goes that the two warring Norse factions spat into a vat to seal their truce and, from the spit, a man was fashioned who became the wisest man on Earth— Kvasir. Unfortunately, Kvasir should have been wise enough to refuse a dinner invitation from Fjalar and Galar…

ACTUAL SIZE

▶ HAVING KILLED KVASIR, THE DWARVES CAUGHT HIS BLOOD AND MIXED IT WITH HONEY to make a potent mead. To their delight, everyone who drank the mead was granted the gift of poetry, and the dwarves soon become very rich. Not content with their new-found wealth, however, the dwarves continued their murderous ways, killing the frost giant Gillingr and his wife. Gillingr's son Suttungr eventually caught the scheming pair, who agreed to give him the poet's mead if he would spare their lives.

Where in the world?

Snorri Sturluson was an Icelandic poet and historian. His tales were based on Old Norse myths and folk stories, gathered from all over Scandinavia.

● SCANDINAVIA

Did you know?

• As the tale continues, the Norse god Odin decides to steal the poet's wine, which the giant hides in the heart of a mountain. In snake form, Odin slithers inside to discover that Suttungr's daughter, Gunnlöð, is guarding the precious liquor. Gunnlöð is charmed by Odin and allows him three sips of the mead in return for three nights in his company. Odin breaks his oath and steals all of the mead. In the poem "Hávamál," however, it is said that Odin regrets deceiving "her proud and passionate heart."

• Kvasir's blood is magical and the dwarves use three special vessels to contain it. These are Són, Boðn, and the kettle Óðrerir.

• According to the English author Kevin Crossley-Holland, the name "Kvasir" comes from the Russian word *kvas*, which is a type of fermented drink similar to beer but stronger.

Gudanna
(*Good-anna*)

HORNS
The gods made Gudanna so beautifully that his horns were coated with layers of lapis lazuli (a deep-blue precious stone).

BREATH
The bull's breath is so poisonous that just one snort is said to be able to kill a hundred warriors.

POWER
Gudanna is no ordinary bull. He is described in *The Epic of Gilgamesh* as "the Bull of Heaven," with divine strength and power.

BODY
Gudanna appears in the form of a magnificent, giant bull. Many ancient people and cultures worshipped bulls in some form.

Heroes have a knack for finding trouble, and none more so than Gilgamesh. While washing in a stream, Gilgamesh attracts the attention of Inanna, the goddess of love and war. She is so taken by the handsome hero that she offers him a chariot, palaces, and rule over all men if he will be her husband. Inanna is beautiful but terrifying, and

Gilgamesh refuses. In a fury, the goddess begs her father to let loose Gudanna, the Bull of Heaven, to kill Gilgamesh. At first he refuses, but Inanna threatens to open the gates of the underworld until the dead outnumber the living. So, reluctantly, he agrees.

ACTUAL SIZE

▶ THE CITY OF URUK TREMBLED AS, BELLOWING AND SNORTING, the great bull roars down from the sky. As it lands, a crack opens in the earth, swallowing up a hundred of the city's bravest warriors. Gudanna has arrived! With a smile, Inanna moves to its side and whispers into the beast's upturned ear. Even now she feels raw rage at the mention of the name "Gilgamesh." She will have her revenge against the arrogant hero and Gudanna will be the instrument of that revenge.

Did you know?

● Gilgamesh's sword brother, Enkidu, catches Gudanna by the tail. Gilgamesh then strikes the killing blow. Later, Enkidu brandishes Gudanna's butchered remains at the goddess Inanna, threatening to do the same to her if she does not leave the city. For daring to challenge the gods, Enkidu is killed and Gilgamesh loses his best friend.

● *The Epic of Gilgamesh* is perhaps the world's oldest story, written between 2750 and 600 BC. It was written on twelve clay tablets, discovered by Hormuzd Rassam in 1853 in the remains of the Royal Library of Ashurbanipal, Iraq.

● The eleventh tablet tells a version of the Old Testament flood story. When it was identified in 1872 by George Smith at the British Museum, he "rushed about the room in a great state of excitement, and, to the astonishment of those present, began to undress himself."

Where in the world?

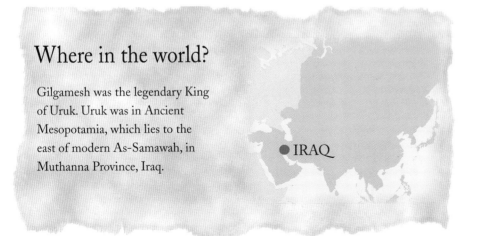

Gilgamesh was the legendary King of Uruk. Uruk was in Ancient Mesopotamia, which lies to the east of modern As-Samawah, in Muthanna Province, Iraq.

● IRAQ

Gulon

(*Goo-lon*)

FUR
Gulon fur is described as "brown-black … like damask cloth…. Princes and great men use this fur in winter."

BODY
This odd creature has the body of a dog, the claws of a cat, and the shaggy coat and bushy tail of a fox.

TEETH
The Gulon is a carnivore (meat-eater). It has sharp claws and teeth designed to cut and tear flesh.

BELLY
The Gulon is famously greedy. Its belly is able to stretch to accommodate the huge portions of meat it consumes.

Is it a bear? An Arctic fox? Or a wild cat? The Gulon looks like some crazy mash-up of Scandinavia's most feared predators. With the face and claws of a cat, the body of a dog, the coat of a fox, and the build of a bear, the Gulon is known and feared throughout northern Europe. However, it is not its appearance that has made the Gulon so infamous, but its eating habits! This legendary beast is famously greedy, known for gorging on meat until it is too full to move! It isn't a fussy eater, either. The Gulon is happy to make a meal of leftovers or go out hunting for something fresher!

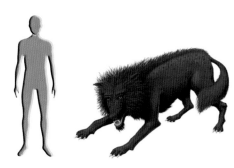

ACTUAL SIZE

▶ "AMONGST ALL THE CREATURES THAT ARE THOUGHT TO BE INSATIABLE in the Northern parts of Sweden, the Gulo [is] the principal … this creature is the most voracious, for when it finds a carcass, he devours so much that his body … is so full of meat that it is stretched like a drum … [Then] finding a strait passage between trees, he presseth between them, that he may discharge [empty] his body by violence." (From Olaus Magnus, *History of the Northern People*.)

Where in the world?

Tales of this creature are told throughout Scandinavia, Germany, and Russia. According to Olaus Magnus, the Gulon lives on the "Northern Snowfields."

● RUSSIA
● SCANDINAVIA
● GERMANY

Did you know?

• According to Olaus Magnus, if someone wears Gulon skins or uses them as blankets for warmth they take on aspects of the creature's personality, especially its appetite: "… when men sleep under the skins they have dreams which agree with the nature of the creature and have an insatiable stomach … [which] seems never to be satisfied."

• Hunters were said to drink the Gulon's blood mixed with hot water. Seasoned with honey, it was a popular drink at weddings because of its aphrodisiac properties!

• Magnus says that the Gulon is known as a Jerff in northern Sweden.

• It is possible that the Gulon is based on the real-life wolverine, which is a powerful hunter and scavenger. The wolverine's Latin name is *Gulo gulo* due to its voracious appetite. (*Gulo* is Latin for glutton.)

Hedammu

(*Hed-a-moo*)

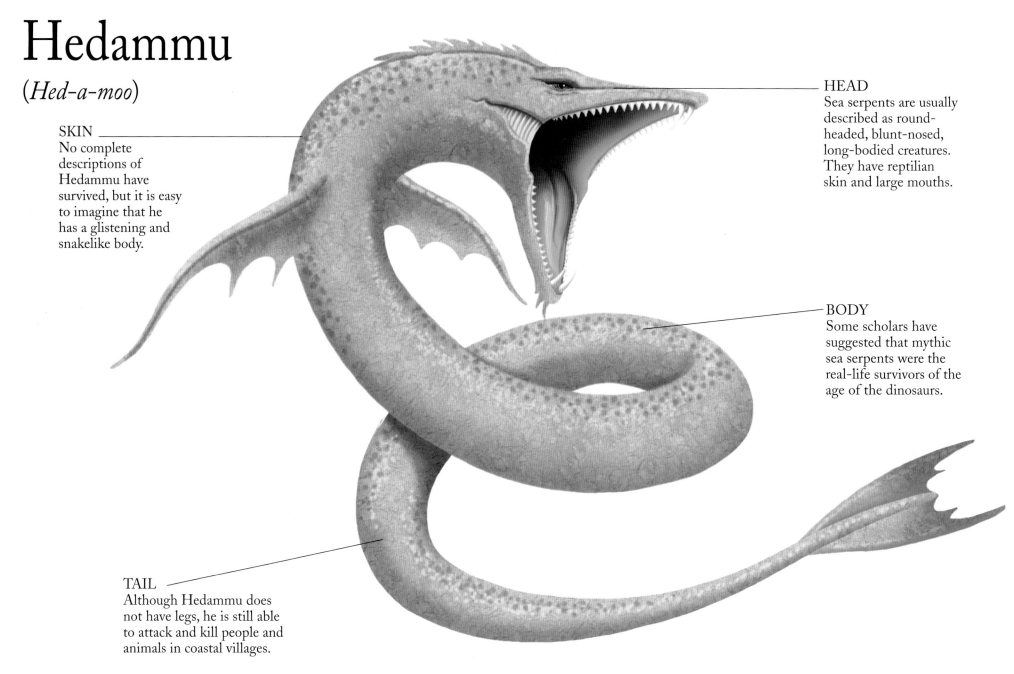

SKIN
No complete descriptions of Hedammu have survived, but it is easy to imagine that he has a glistening and snakelike body.

HEAD
Sea serpents are usually described as round-headed, blunt-nosed, long-bodied creatures. They have reptilian skin and large mouths.

BODY
Some scholars have suggested that mythic sea serpents were the real-life survivors of the age of the dinosaurs.

TAIL
Although Hedammu does not have legs, he is still able to attack and kill people and animals in coastal villages.

For this titanic sea serpent, the ocean is just one huge, mobile feast. However, Hedammu isn't content to simply eat what the seas have to offer. He has a huge appetite and he has discovered that there is plenty of tasty food on the land, too. After spending the day gorging himself, the serpent rises from the sea one more time to cast a baleful eye at the nearby coastal village. Even now his belly isn't full... The villagers, seeing his monstrous head rise from the waves, call out to the goddess Ishtar for aid and protection. Ishtar is the goddess of love and was both a beautiful and a deadly opponent...

ACTUAL SIZE

▶ ON HEARING THE PEOPLE'S CRIES, ISHTAR DRESSES IN HER FINEST CLOTHES and smears herself with perfumed oil. Heading for the shore, she calls out to the serpent, using all her charm to persuade Hedammu to leave the villagers in peace. Hedammu looks at the goddess but his hunger makes him see Ishtar as nothing but a tasty snack. Casting a spell, Ishtar turns the ocean into a sleeping potion, leaving the great serpent drowsy and much more susceptible to her charms.

Where in the world?

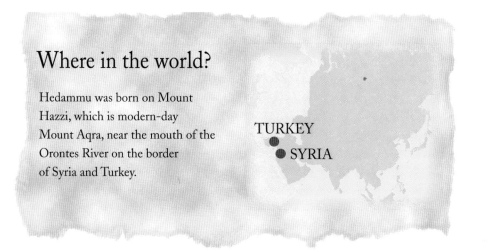

Hedammu was born on Mount Hazzi, which is modern-day Mount Aqra, near the mouth of the Orontes River on the border of Syria and Turkey.

TURKEY

SYRIA

Did you know?

• The Bronze Age (c. 3300–1200 BC) tale known as "The Kingship of Heaven" tells the story of a battle between Kumarbi, the chief god of the Huttians, and his son, the weather god, Tešub. It is in this cycle of stories that "The Myth of the Dragon Hedammu" appears. Sadly, only sixteen fragments of the tale survive. These were found in Hittite translations on clay tablets in the royal archives at Boğazköy in modern-day Turkey.

• The very earliest civilizations worshipped female creator goddesses. Ishtar and Inanna (see the entry for Gudanna) are versions of the same goddess.

• Hedammu is the son of the chief god Kumarbi and the daughter of the sea god, Sertapsuruhi. He has a brother who is a giant stone monster called Ullikummi. Ullikummi's mother was a female cliff!

Herensuge

(*Her-en-soo-gay*)

HEADS
Legends about this abominable dragon vary. In some, Herensuge has seven heads. In some tales he has just one.

MOUTH
This big beast has many mouths to feed! Its heads snap and writhe in anticipation as potential food comes close.

BODY
In most legends told about this fantastical beast it can fly, although, like Chinese dragons, it does not have wings.

APPEARANCE
The "suge" part of Herensuge's name means "snake" in the Basque language, but this beast is generally considered to be a dragon.

I n Basque legends, there are numerous tales about Herensuge, a seven-headed dragon that gorges on cattle and people with equal gusto. However, the story of Teodosio of Goñi is the most famous story. In it, Teodosio, a noble knight, is tricked by the devil into murdering his own parents. He then travels to Rome to beg the pope for forgiveness.

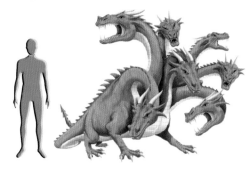

ACTUAL SIZE

The pope decides that Teodosio should be wrapped in chains and forced to wander the land. Only when the chains work loose will he have atoned for his terrible crime. Returning from Rome and still bound in chains, Teodosio encounters Herensuge…

▶ THE VILLAGERS OF LARRAÚN WERE SO TERRIFIED THAT EVERY YEAR they offered Herensuge a sacrifice to ensure their safety. Discovering a young victim bound, like himself, in chains, Teodosio cries out to Saint Michael. He vows that if the Archangel will free him from his bindings, he will fight the beast. As the battle rages, the knight stumbles to the ground. The dragon closes, but Teodosio raises his sword, making the shape of the cross. The beast falls back and Teodosio slays him.

Where in the world?

This myth comes from the ancient kingdom of Navarre, in the Basque region of Spain. Herensuge was said to inhabit the mountain ranges of the region.

● SPAIN

Did you know?

• Many folk tales contain elements of truth. At the end of the tale, Teodosio returns home and builds a church to Saint Michael. The real-life sanctuary church of San Miguel in Excelsis is on the Sierra of Aralar, just below the peak of Mount Artxueta, close to the village of Larraún. It dates from the period of the legend.

• While many legends keep the details vague, the story of Teodosio and Herensuge is surprisingly specific. It places the events in Navarre, in the year 707 AD, and gives the name of the knight's wife as Constance of Butron.

• Herensuge is also known as Herren-Surge or Herensugue.

• The story of Teodosio and Herensuge appears in a famous romantic historical novel published in 1879 by Francisco Navarro-Villoslada. The novel is called *Amaya and Basques in the Eighth Century*.

Huli-Jing
(*Ho-lee-jing*)

AGE
In the story "Fengshen Yanyi" (meaning "The Investiture of the Gods"), Huli-Jing is an extremely powerful 1,000-year-old vixen spirit.

BODY
In Chinese myths any animal can acquire the ability to shape-shift. Huli-Jing often transforms itself into a beautiful woman.

TAILS
In Asia, fox spirits gain a new tail and increase their power every 100 years until they reach the full nine tails.

SIZE
There are no records of how large Huli-Jing is, but nature spirits are often much larger than their real-life counterparts.

It is no surprise that ancient people were afraid of the dark and the beasts that lurk in it. Folk tales often tell stories about real animals that are supernaturally big or powerful. In the case of the fox, legends seem to agree that this is one cunning creature! Foxes are known to be clever hunters, and their mythical counterparts are often portrayed as tricksters or devious shape-shifters. Huli-Jing is a fox spirit from China, but is it a fox in human form, or a human with a foxy spirit? Depending on the tale, it can be both—and both are equally dangerous. In the 16th-century tale "Fengshen Yanyi," a woman is possessed by a fox spirit…

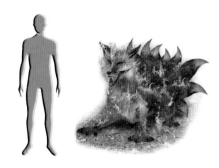

ACTUAL SIZE

▶ DAJI MIGHT HAVE LOOKED BEAUTIFUL, BUT INSIDE HER RAGED AN ANGRY SPIRIT. Daji's husband, the Emperor Zhou Xin, had offended the goddess Nüwa, who sent Huli-Jing to expel Daji's soul from her body and take control. Using Daji's influence, the fox pushed the tyrannical emperor into ever-greater acts of oppression and cruelty. Finally, the emperor's generals revolted and the defeated Zhou Xin retreated to his palace, gathered his treasures around him, and set the palace alight. Thus was a dynasty toppled and a goddess avenged.

Where in the world?

Huli-Jing is a creature from Chinese mythology. Such myths often contain fictionalized accounts of real events and are a valuable insight into the ancient Chinese world.

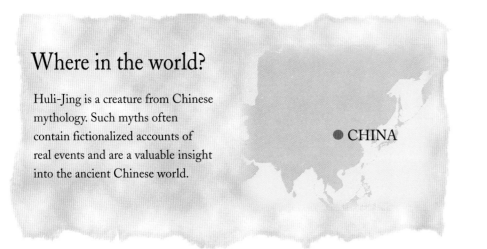

● CHINA

Did you know?

● Huli-Jing is one of three spirits that the goddess Nüwa sends to hasten the evil emperor's downfall. As well as Huli-Jing she sends a nine-headed pheasant (Jiutou Zhiji Jing) and a jade pippa spirit (Pipa Jing). These spirits are like the mischievous fairies in Western folk tales. At the end of "Fengshen Yanyi," however, Huli-Jing is punished by Nüwa, as the goddess's instructions were to bewitch the emperor but not to cause harm to others.

● The *Book of Zhou*, which is an official history of the Zhou Dynasty completed in 636 AD, depicts the nine-tailed fox as a beast of good luck and peace.

● Korean legends tell of a fox spirit called a Gumiho that has a taste for human blood.

● The fox spirit always appears in the form of a beautiful woman.

Hundun

(*Hoon-doon*)

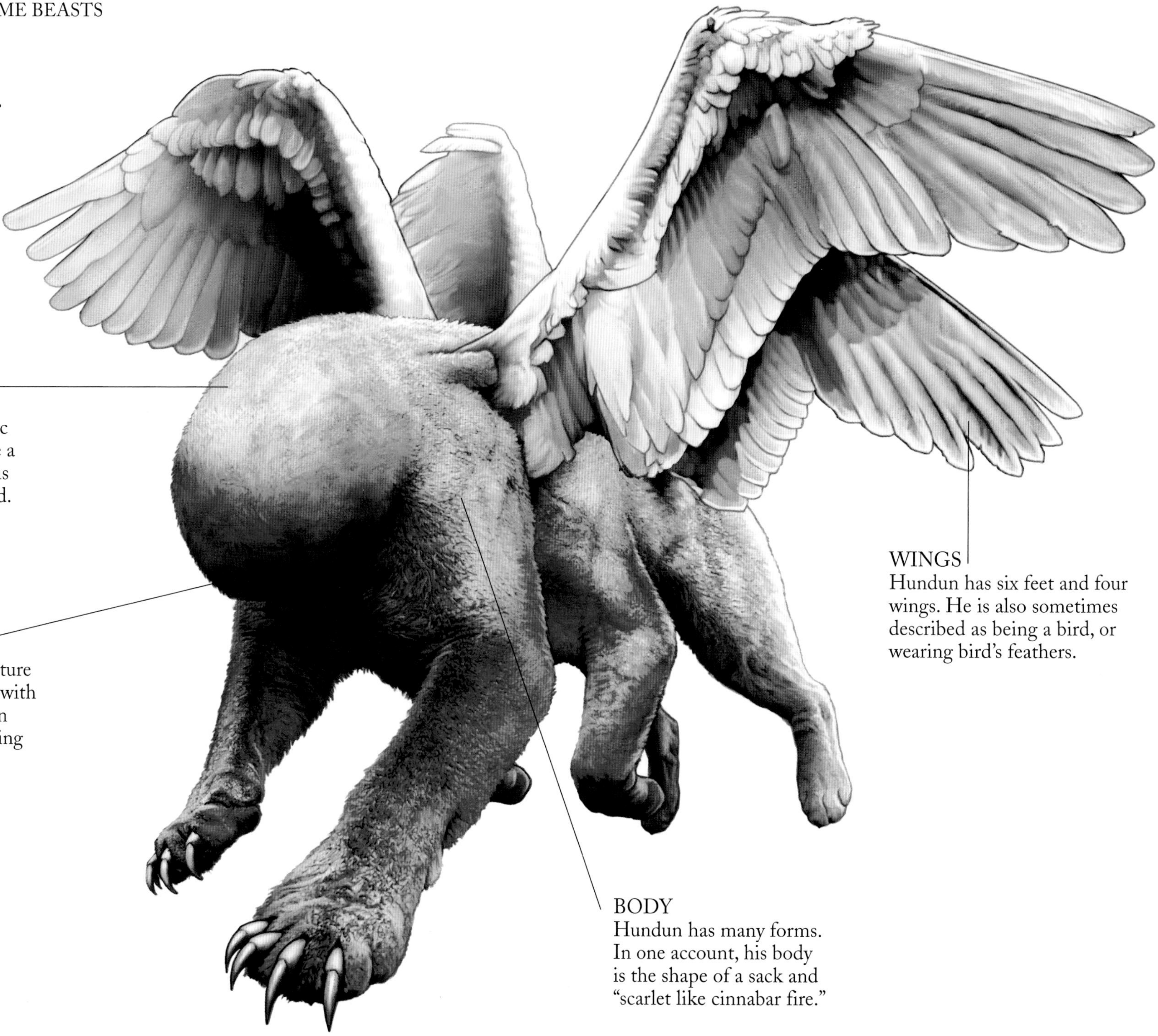

HEAD
With no face and
no eyes, the chaotic
Hundun looks like a
beast whose body is
only partly finished.

MOUTH
Although this creature
is often illustrated with
no mouth, Hundun
is said to love to "sing
and dance."

WINGS
Hundun has six feet and four
wings. He is also sometimes
described as being a bird, or
wearing bird's feathers.

BODY
Hundun has many forms.
In one account, his body
is the shape of a sack and
"scarlet like cinnabar fire."

Hundun is a lumpen, half-formed beast from Chinese creation myths. In some tales he is little more than a blob. He exists without a head, eyes, hands, or feet, and makes noises like thunder in the darkness. In some tales, he is a vicious and stupid dog with long hair, who sits on Heaven Mountain, repeatedly chasing his own tail. In other tales, he is a creator spirit, with six feet and four wings, no face, and no eyes. Whatever this beast's true appearance, one thing is certain: He is a creature of chaos and confusion for anyone who encounters him.

ACTUAL SIZE

▶ WHENZHI STAGGERED BACK IN HORROR. The creature before him reared its strange half-formed legs, punching the air as its wings flapped furiously. The monstrosity had no eyes, and no mouth, but it still seemed to be looking directly at the terrified merchant. Whenzhi prided himself on being well-educated. He had read about such creatures, of course, but he had always dismissed such folk stories as tales told to sell cheap art prints and keep peasants awake at night.

Where in the world?

Hundun legends date from the Warring States period of Ancient China. These wars ended with China being unified for the first time in 221 BC.

● CHINA

Did you know?

● In Chinese creation myths, Hundun is also the name given to the chaos out of which the thunder egg that contained the world grew. Inside the egg is the god Pangu. When the egg hatches, the two halves of the egg become the earth and the sky.

● Wonton dumplings get their name from a corruption of the word *hundun*. The shape of the dumplings is said to reflect the blobs of chaotic matter that Chinese myths suggest were present at the start of creation.

● In *Pacific Rim*, the 2013 American science fiction movie directed by Guillermo del Toro, Hundun is the name of the second Kaiju to attack Earth. The beast attacks the Philippine capital. He is ultimately defeated.

● In the platform game *The Legend of Korra*, Hundun is an avatar trapped in the Spirit World.

Hydrus
(*Hy-druss*)

FLIGHT
In many legends, dragons and serpents can fly although they have no wings. Hydrus, though, seems to be land-bound.

HEAD
The Hydrus has just one head. It is often confused with the Hydra, which had many heads that could be regrown.

BODY
Usually described as snakelike, the Hydrus has no set appearance. Ancient authors compared it to a bird, an otter, and a dragon.

MALE
The name "Hydrus" comes from a Greek word meaning "male water snake." A female water snake is called a Hydra.

Medieval scholars loved making books of the world's beasts. These volumes were the popular natural history of the age and included "imaginary" animals like hippos and "real" creatures like dragons and unicorns! The Hydrus appears in many such books, but the roots of this legend go back much, much earlier.

In Ancient Egypt, the Hydrus was said to be the enemy of the crocodile. Whenever the two beasts met, they fought. The crocodile would always overpower the snake, swallowing it, but Hydrus would eat its way out of the crocodile's stomach, killing its enemy.

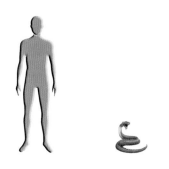

ACTUAL SIZE

▶ "ENHYDROS [THE HYDRUS] IS A LITTLE BEAST … named from the fact that it dwells in the waters … most of all in the Nile. … if these beasts find a crocodile sleeping, he revolves itself in the mud … and enters the crocodile by its mouth…. Once inside the crocodile's belly, it eats all of its insides, so the crocodile dies…. It is called an *ichneumon* [mongoose] in Greek because it has the look and smell of that beast." (Translation from Isidore of Seville's *Etymologies*.)

Where in the world?

It is likely that Hydrus originated in Lower Egypt, at the sites of the cult of Uto at the twinned cities of Pe and Dep.

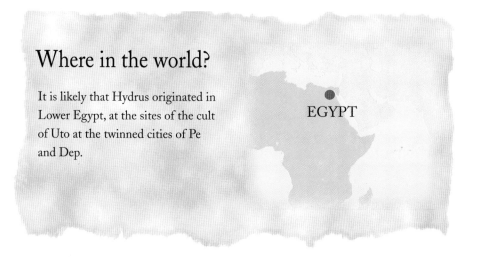

EGYPT

Did you know?

• For Ancient Egyptians, the tale of Enhydros or the Hydrus symbolized the battle between darkness and light. Egyptians were sun worshippers, so this may have been the perceived daily battle between the sun to drive away the night, or a symbolic battle between good and evil.

• In Medieval books of imagined animals, known as bestiaries, every creature was said to be the creation of the Christian God and each had a symbolic meaning. The story of the Hydrus was therefore adopted as a symbol of rebirth, as the water snake is reborn from the belly of the crocodile.

• Saint Isidore of Seville (c. 560–636 AD) says in his *Etymologies* that Hydrus is an aquatic snake that some call a "*boa…* because [its bite] is remedied with cow (*bos*) dung."

• The constellation of Hydrus is in the southern hemisphere. Its counterpart, Hydra, is the largest constellation in the southern sky.

Ilomba

(*Ee-lom-ba*)

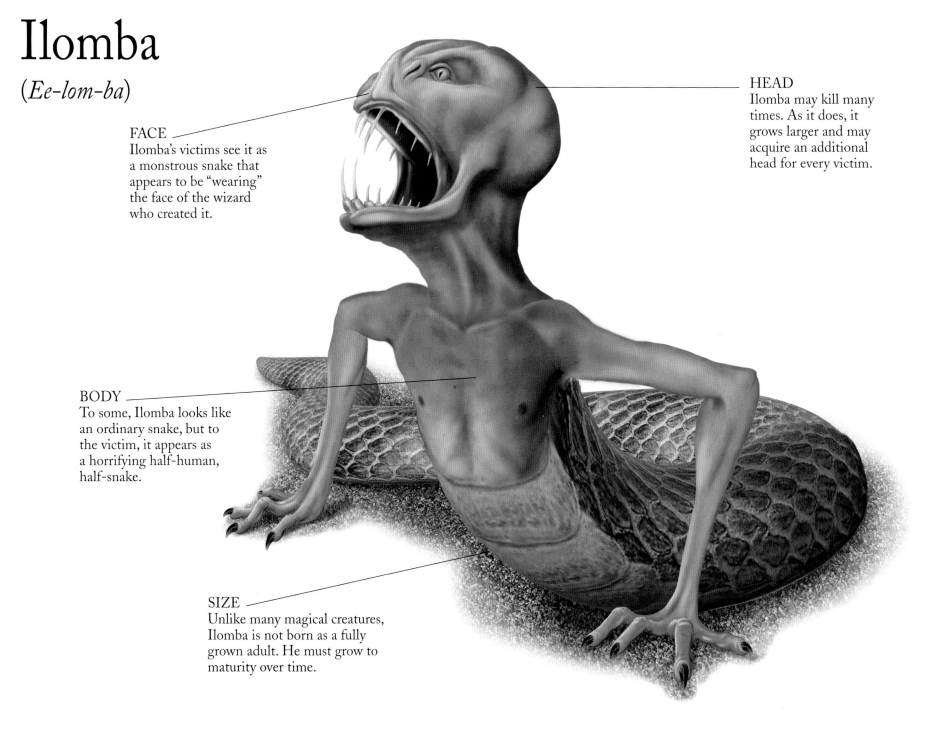

FACE
Ilomba's victims see it as
a monstrous snake that
appears to be "wearing"
the face of the wizard
who created it.

HEAD
Ilomba may kill many
times. As it does, it
grows larger and may
acquire an additional
head for every victim.

BODY
To some, Ilomba looks like
an ordinary snake, but to
the victim, it appears as
a horrifying half-human,
half-snake.

SIZE
Unlike many magical creatures,
Ilomba is not born as a fully
grown adult. He must grow to
maturity over time.

All was quiet inside the house. It was night now, and the only occupant was drifting in and out of sleep. Suddenly there was a rustle, as though someone—or something—was pushing its way through the reedwork roof. There in the moonlight was a sight that made the room's occupant howl in terror. Dropping through the roof into the room was a gigantic snake, but what had made the man cry out wasn't the sight of the reptile. It was the creature's monstrous face! Even when horribly distorted, he recognized the beast's features immediately. It was the face of the wizard Mukelabai, and the Ilomba was here to kill him!

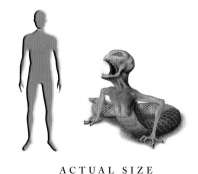

ACTUAL SIZE

▶ THE WIZARD MUKELABAI HAD CREATED THE ILOMBA from the blood and nails of his enemies, sealed in snakeskin and brought to life by magic. At first the Ilomba had been nothing more than an egg. Slowly it had hatched and started to grow, fed on a diet of porridge and eggs. Now, after five years, it was old enough to demand victims and Mukelabai was able to send it out to drink the blood and souls of his enemies.

Where in the world?

The tale of the Ilomba comes from the legends of the Lozi people. The Lozi live in Western Zambia, Namibia, Angola, and Botswana in Africa.

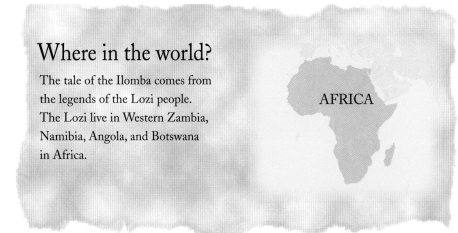

AFRICA

Did you know?

• Like a vampire, Ilomba bites its victim's neck and sucks out the blood. The souls it consumes along with the blood are used by the evil wizard to create zombies—undead slaves!

• This nightmare creature can only live as long as the wizard has victims to feed it. Once that supply is exhausted then the Ilomba will turn on its creator.

• If the wizard is injured or killed, then so is the Ilomba. The same is true of the Ilomba. The wizard can destroy his creation, but once he does so he is forever haunted by the souls of those he has murdered.

• In November 2012, the *Zambian Watchdog* newspaper printed a letter from a police officer. The officer wanted to report the behavior of a corrupt fellow officer who was believed to be keeping an Ilomba at the police station.

Jorōgumo
(Jolo–go–mo)

AGE
In Asian myths, animals become more powerful as they get older. When spiders turn 400 years old, they gain magical powers.

SIZE
Jorōgumo is a shape-shifter. She can change her size and her appearance, growing as large as a horse in some accounts.

SPINNERETS
Just like real spiders, Jorōgumo spins threads of silk with which to build webs and capture unsuspecting prey.

BODY
Jorōgumo is usually portrayed as either a beautiful young woman or as a creature that is half-spider and half-woman.

If legends are to be believed, in Japan attractive women should be feared rather than admired! Jorōgumo is a Yōkai, a supernatural monster with the ability to bewitch. Jorōgumo is a giant spider spirit who uses shape-shifting magic to catch a meal. Sometimes Jorōgumo transforms herself into an empty house and simply sits in wait for weary travelers to step inside! But most often she takes the form of a lovely young lady, who charms travelers with music, food, sake, and pleasing company. Come too close, though, and Jorōgumo strikes—wrapping her victims up in webs of silk, then devouring them at her leisure.

ACTUAL SIZE

▶ THE RAIN HIT HIM LIKE AN ICY BLANKET. The nearest village was still far away and the traveler jogged miserably toward the light in the distance. As he got closer, he heard singing. Closer still and he could see the small house where, through the open door, he spied a beautiful woman playing on a *biwa*. The traveler had passed this way many times but had never noticed the house before. But it was dark and cold, and the house looked warm and inviting…

Where in the world?

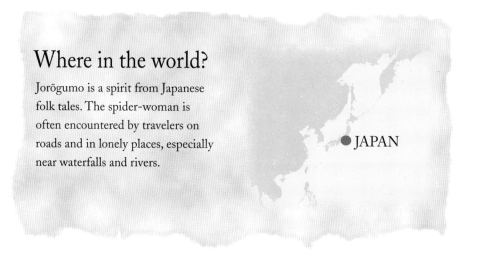

Jorōgumo is a spirit from Japanese folk tales. The spider-woman is often encountered by travelers on roads and in lonely places, especially near waterfalls and rivers.

●JAPAN

Did you know?

● In *Tsuchigumo Soushi*, written in the 14th century, the real-life Minamoto no Raikō is the hero of a tale involving another spider spirit called Tsuchigumo. When Minamoto finally tracks the monster spider to her lair, he cuts her open and the heads of 1,990 villagers topple from her stomach!

● Tales about Jorōgumo first appear in stories from the Edo Period (1603–1868). In many, Jorōgumo is a spider who can change her appearance into a beautiful woman. However, one of the most famous illustrations of Jorōgumo comes from *Gazu Hyakki Yagyō* ("The Illustrated Night Parade of One Hundred Demons"). Published in 1776, illustrator Toriyama Sekien's supernatural book remains hugely popular. Sekien's depictions of ghosts, spirits, and demons include Jorōgumo, who is shown as half-woman, half-spider. The illustrator's work still influences the look of supernatural creatures in many Japanese films and animations.

Kee-Wakw

(*Kee-wok-a*)

VOICE
The cry of the Kee-Wakw can kill those who hear it. The female Kiwakweskwa makes a noise like a roaring lion.

HEART
In place of his heart the Kee-Wakw has a piece of ice in his chest, in the shape of a man.

BODY
This beast is constantly hungry. His body is emaciated and he is so hungry that he has eaten his own lips!

SEX
The female Kee-Wakw is sometimes referred to as Kiwakweskwa. She is more powerful, and more deadly, than the male.

Kee-Wakw, Giwakwa, Chenoo… Among the native peoples of North America, this evil frost giant is known by many names. Although his body is emaciated, Kee-Wakw is large and lethal. Once human, Kee-Wakw's heart was turned to ice when he committed an unspeakable crime. Now, he is condemned to wander the frozen forests of the continent, looking for food to sate his constant hunger. The bad news is that Kee-Wakw is a man-eater who consumes the souls as well as the flesh of those he eats. For every person this horror devours, he gains an additional icy heart shaped like the body of his victim!

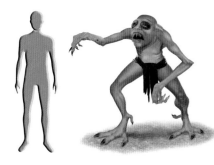

ACTUAL SIZE

▶ FOR AS LONG AS KEE-WAKW COULD REMEMBER he had been wracked by hunger. No matter how much he ate, his belly growled and his body grew thinner. Once, a long time ago, Kee-Wakw hadn't been Kee-Wakw. He had been an ordinary man, but he still remembered the hunger of that last winter. He remembered how hunger had pushed him to steal food from his own children. He knew he was being punished for that now, but instead of regret, he felt only hunger. That was all he ever felt.

Where in the world?

Kee-Wakw appears in native legends throughout northern North America. He is especially associated with the Wabanaki, Algonquian, Passamaquoddy, and Abenaki peoples.

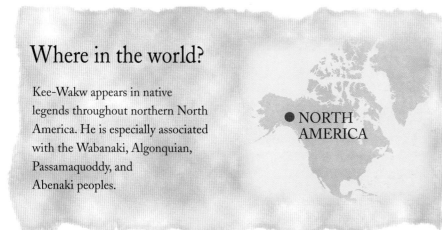

● NORTH AMERICA

Did you know?

● According to Frank Speck's 1935 article "Penobscot Tales and Religious Beliefs," the word *kiwakwa* means "going about in the woods."

● In Passamaquoddy tales, the Kee-Wakw's heart is said to be an ice shard in the shape of a man. This human figure is Kee-Wakw's soul. When he kills, Kee-Wakw adds another frozen soul to his own. Kee-Wakw's strength therefore depends upon the number or the size of the ice shards that make up his heart. If the Kee-Wakw's icy heart is removed, then he can become human again.

● Kee-Wakw may look half-starved, but in a fight he grows to immense size, uprooting trees to use as clubs.

● Kee-Wakw doesn't wear clothes, but in the summer he rubs himself with fir balsam and rolls on the ground, so that his body becomes covered in moss and leaves.

Koschei the Deathless

(Ko-shay the Deathless)

BONY
There are no definite descriptions of this beast, but Koschei comes from the Russian meaning "bone," suggesting that he has a skeletal appearance.

POWER
Starved-looking, with skin as thin as paper, Koschei's body may look fragile but it is fueled by powerful evil forces.

SIZE
Koschei appears in hundreds of Eastern European legends. In some, he is portrayed as a dragon. In others he is a giant.

BODY
According to accounts, Koschei looks like a lich (an undead creature). Long hair and clawlike nails add to his corpselike appearance.

High in his castle, Koschei sits in gloomy contemplation. The wizard's wickedness had given him everything he could ever want. After many years of secret study and monstrous experimentation, his magic is so powerful that no feat of sorcery is beyond him. He can change his appearance. He can fly at great speed. He can enchant any woman he desires. He can kill anyone who dares to cross him with the merest spell. However, one thing is still beyond his control. Like all mortals, Koschei knows that he will die one day. Or will he? Even now the wizard has a plan for escaping his final fate.

A C T U A L   S I Z E

► TO ESCAPE DEATH, KOSCHEI SEPARATES HIS SOUL FROM HIS BODY and hides it inside a needle. He places the needle inside an egg, inside a duck, inside a hare. The hare is hidden in an iron chest, buried under an oak tree on the mythical Island of Buyan. The island itself blinks in and out of existence. Anyone wishing to kill Koschei must find and open the chest, retrieve the egg from the body of the duck, and smash it open on Koschei's forehead!

Where in the world?

Koschei the Deathless is a popular villain in Eastern European tales. He is particularly associated with Russian, Polish, and Czech folk stories.

EASTERN EUROPE

Did you know?

● Although Koschei is called "immortal" and "deathless," it may be more accurate to describe him as "undead," as popular illustrations of him always give him a corpselike appearance.

● The folk tale "The Firebird" tells how Prince Ivan Tsarevitch defeats the evil Koschei. In the tale the warrior queen, Marya Morevna, holds Koschei captive in her castle. She is in love with Prince Ivan, but when he accidentally frees the wizard, Koschei abducts her. Ivan must enter the evil wizard's magical realm to free her. At the end of the tale, the two are married and their kingdoms are united. The tale inspired the *Firebird* ballet suite by Igor Stravinsky.

● Koschei is the name used by an early incarnation of the evil Time Lord, The Master, in the *Doctor Who* novels *The Dark Path* and *Face of the Enemy*.

Krasue
(*Kra-soo*)

HEAD
In some stories, the head appears on its own. In others, the organs of the body hang below the Krasue's neck.

TEETH
Krasue is often portrayed in modern films as having a pair of pointed fangs.

MOUTH
The Krasue has a big appetite and loves to feast on the flesh and blood of domestic animals and humans.

GLOW
The eerie-looking Krasue consists of a floating head surrounded by flickering ghost lights, which are often compared to a will-o'-the-wisp.

The Krasue is a creature created by magic and fueled by death and destruction. Despite having no body to feed, the creature is a glutton who spends its evenings in search of fresh meat and blood to satisfy its hunger. Cattle and pets are easy prey for this supernatural hunter, but she also has more alarming tastes. In parts of Thailand, it is believed that Krasue preys on pregnant women. Thorns are placed around the homes of any expectant mothers to protect the unborn baby and drive the disembodied head away. Despite her horrific nature, Krasue is a popular figure in South Asian fiction. She has even featured in a Thai soap opera.

ACTUAL SIZE

▶ KOSAL LOVED HORROR STORIES AND LOVED BEING SCARED. His favorite thing was to watch a late-night horror movie with salty snacks and fizzy drinks. It made him laugh to think that, in his mother's village, there were people who really believed in ghosts and evil spirits. One old man he knew even claimed to have been visited by a Krasue! Kosal had laughed at that, but, as his mother pointed out, he did still watch movies with the lights on!

Where in the world?

Tales of the Krasue are popular throughout Southeast Asia, including Cambodia, Indonesia, Laos, Malaysia, and Thailand. The name is slightly different in each country.

SOUTHEAST ASIA

Did you know?

● In some stories, the Krasue has a body that she keeps hidden while she goes hunting. If the Krasue fails to return to her body before the morning, or if her body is damaged, then the Krasue will be destroyed.

● The Indonesian Leyak, Malaysian Penanggalan, and the Cambodian Arp are similar to the Krasue and appear in other South Asian tales. As well as having the ability to separate their head from their body, these beasts are all female.

● The Manananggal from Philippine myths can separate its whole torso from its lower body. Its upper half then sprouts bat wings and sets off to do mischief. Like vampires, it is vulnerable to salt, garlic, and sunlight. Some Manananggals are male.

● One beast is bad, but two are even worse! Krasue often appears alongside a male spirit, which is called a Krahang.

Lampalugua

(*Lamp-a-lug-oo-a*)

BODY
The Lampalugua's body is described as being dusty red in color, perhaps similar to the real-life anaconda.

SKIN
It is an aquatic creature, so it is likely that Lampalugua's skin is like a crocodile's—waterproof with armored "scutes" (scales).

EYES
With eyes on the side of its head, Lampalugua doesn't have binocular vision like most predators, but it compensates with raw power.

CLAWS
The beast's oversized claws make impressive weapons. Combined with its jaws and muscular build, these weapons give its victims little chance of escape.

This monster from Chile is both big and bad! The Lampalugua is a muscular reptile with an appetite to match its size. Devouring everything and anything in its path, Lampalugua has a formidable reputation. In local legends, it is said to drink rivers dry, trample crops, and chew up cattle and people with ease. When it is not on the rampage, it stays cool by digging itself a shallow underground cavern in which to rest. There it lurks unseen, until hunger strikes again and it heads off to find itself another monster-sized meal.

ACTUAL SIZE

▶ WHENEVER ANYONE ASKED RAPIMAN if he could get them some water from the stream, he would make an excuse. He made so many excuses that the villagers joked that he was afraid someone might give him a bath! However, to Rapiman, it was no joke. He knew that a Lampalugua lived near the stream. Once, many years ago, he had narrowly escaped becoming its dinner. Now he was convinced that the beast had his scent and would gobble him up if it got the chance.

Where in the world?

These tales come from Chile's Araucanian people who now live in the valleys and basins of South Central Chile from the Biobío to the Toltén River.

CHILE

Did you know?

• In the 1900s, a Chilean folklorist called Sperata de Saunière recorded a "true" tale from a native Araucanian woman. The woman told her of a mysterious animal that had been eating a rich man's sheep. The creature was an enormous reptile, like a serpent with the head of a wild cat. On the tip of its tongue was a nail that carried poison, like a snake's fangs. The native woman referred to the beast as Lampalugua.

• Lampalugua comes from the myths of the Araucanian people. Another of their tales concerns Guecubu—a demon that can fill fields with crop-destroying caterpillars, bring disease to cattle, and eat up all the fish in a river.

• In Argentina, the local name for the boa constrictor is the Lampalagua. The boa constrictor is a large, heavy-bodied snake found in North, Central, and South America.

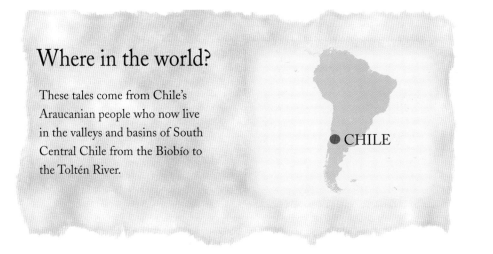

Nian
(Nee-ann)

SKIN
Is the Nian a reptile, or more like a lion? Here, our artist has used many descriptions to produce a "composite" photo-fit beast.

EYES
Like all predators, Nian has eyes at the front of its head, giving it binocular vision—perfect for judging distances.

BODY
Early descriptions compare Nian to a combination of a lion, a unicorn, and an ox. In later depictions, it is more dragonlike.

MOUTH
This mythical beast's gaping mouth is a terrifying sight—filled to the brim with very large and very sharp teeth.

Nian is a monster from ancient Chinese tales who emerges from his lair in the early spring, hungry and looking for easy pickings. In statues, Nian is shown in many guises. In some, he is a combination of a lion, a unicorn, and an ox. In others, he has a shaggy mane and a bearlike body. Over time, images of Nian became more reptilian, until we get the dragon-serpent of the colorful Dragon Dance. If you have ever thrilled to the sight of a Chinese Dragon Dance, then you will know that the tale that inspired it dates back many thousands of years…

ACTUAL SIZE

▶ THE ELDERS KNEW THE BEAST WOULD ATTACK SOON, but this spring they were ready. The creature was fearfully strong but it was just a beast and, like all beasts, it was startled by loud sounds and fire. So, when the creature appeared, the people rushed into the street. They were all wearing flame-red clothes and had dressed their homes with red paper streamers. Some of the people set off firecrackers. The beast fled, howling in terror. The custom of Guo Nian was born.

Where in the world?

This famous creature comes from Chinese mythology. Traditionally, the Nian lives under the sea or in the mountains and comes to the plains to hunt.

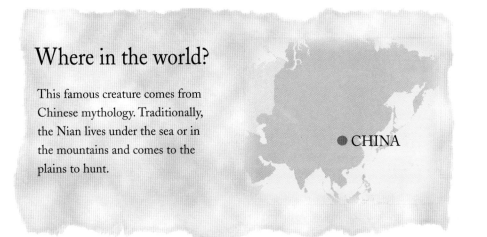

● CHINA

Did you know?

● Guo Nian originally referred to the celebration of "the passing of the beast." Today the phrase means to "celebrate the New Year." (Guo means to "pass over" or "observe.")

● The word "Nian" dates back to the 14th century BC. Originally, the word meant "ripe grains," referring to the harvest that happened at the end of the agricultural year. Eventually, over time, Nian came simply to mean "year." As the beast always attacked at the start of the year, it acquired the same name.

● Chinese New Year is celebrated on the first day of the first month of the Chinese lunar calendar. This means the first day of the second new moon after the day on which the winter solstice occurs.

● In some versions of the legend, a god comes to the aid of the village disguised as an old man.

Peuchen

(Poo-ken)

HEAD
In northern Chile, the flying snake appears on ancient pottery, but it has a head on each end of its body.

EYES
Just one look at the Peuchen's eyes can bring on instant paralysis. This allows Peuchen to suck its victim's blood.

MOUTH
A whistling sound tells people that Peuchen is nearby. No one knows if the sound comes from the creature's mouth or its wings.

WINGS
A pair of feathered wings, or (in some accounts) leathery, batlike wings give this creature mastery of the air.

Over time, some legends fade. Others don't, as proved by an entry in Father Félix de Augusta's Spanish–Mapuche dictionary of 1916. Despite being published in the age of electric lights and cars, the book included mention of a beast whose origins date back to the beginning of the South American Mapuche culture (600–500 BC),

ACTUAL SIZE

and of whom the people were still very much afraid. It had a long, snakelike body, wrote de Augusta, "grows wings and flies" and "sucks the blood of people and animals, drying the body of its victims." Its hissing sound, "piurüt piurüt," announces certain death.

▶ THE EERIE WHISTLE THAT ANNOUNCED THE ARRIVAL OF THE PEUCHEN was unmistakable. While the terrified villagers gathered their families and fled, the Mapuche medicine woman readied herself. It was well known that a Machi such as herself had much power—and that power was based on knowledge. This knowledge told her which herbs to use or which spirits to call on to make her medicine. Now she needed all of that knowledge if she was to defeat the Peuchen.

Where in the world?

This giant flying snake is a creature drawn from the legends of the Mapuche and Chilote peoples who live in south central Chile and southwestern Argentina.

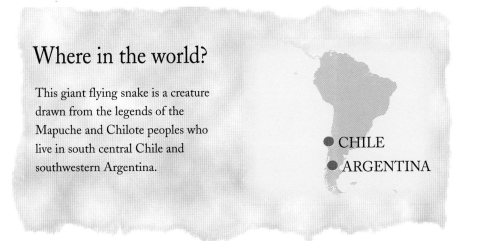

● CHILE
● ARGENTINA

Did you know?

● One of the earliest written references to Peuchen appeared in 1765 in Father Andrés Febrés's *Grammar*. In it he called Peuchen a flying snake.

● It is thought that the origin of the name "Peuchen" or "Piwuchen" comes from *piwu*, meaning "to dry" and *ché* for "person." So "Peuchen" literally means "to dry a person out." This is a reference to Peuchen's habit of drinking human blood.

● Peuchen is also the name given to a real species of vampire bat (*Desmodus rotundus*) found in Mexico, Central, and South America. The bat does indeed feed on blood. It is far too small to be mistaken for a Peuchen, but many scholars think that it could have inspired the myth.

● Some people refer to Peuchen as a vampire as it shares similar abilities to those creatures, such as shape-shifting and drinking blood.

Pukwudgie
(*Puk-wudge-ee*)

EYES
The monster is said to
be able to instill terror
and confuse the minds
of people who look
at it.

BOW
This evil little creature has
quite an arsenal of weapons,
including poison arrows,
poison dust, flint daggers,
and magic!

BODY
Although he can shape-shift,
Pukwudgie most often looks
like a porcupine from the
back, and a dwarfish human
from the front.

SKIN
Pukwudgie's skin is
described as being
smooth gray, which
sometimes glows.

Now you see him, now you don't! Pukwudgie is a troll who can appear and disappear at will. A long time ago, Pukwudgies were harmless creatures, but they became jealous of the affection that the Wampanoag people had for their creator. This jealousy turned into hatred and Pukwudgie began to kidnap children and burn down homes.

ACTUAL SIZE

Pukwudgie is very strong, with the ability to shape-shift and summon fire. But his most chilling power is his ability to control the minds of his victims. Those who survive an encounter with him feel a terror completely out of proportion to the creature's size.

▶ JAMES ALWAYS BOASTED THAT HE HAD A GOOD HEAD FOR HEIGHTS, but for some reason he felt oddly uneasy. He couldn't even really remember walking toward the cliff edge. Perhaps he had been planning to take a photo? Yes, that must be it. He was pulling out his phone to take a snapshot when he felt a prickling sensation on the back of his neck. It was almost as though someone—or something—were creeping up behind him…

Where in the world?

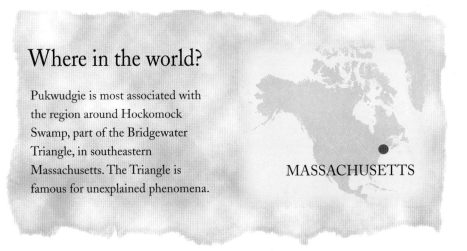

Pukwudgie is most associated with the region around Hockomock Swamp, part of the Bridgewater Triangle, in southeastern Massachusetts. The Triangle is famous for unexplained phenomena.

MASSACHUSETTS

Did you know?

• Pukwudgie means "little man of the wilderness."

• Pukwudgie can also take the form of a bird, insect, dog, or wild cat.

• Bill Russo, a retired iron worker from Raynham, Massachusetts, reported having an unsettling encounter with a small, hairy creature, with eyes like an owl—too big for its head. The creature appeared while Bill and his dog were having their nightly walk close to his home near Hockomock Swamp. Bill reported feeling unnaturally afraid as he listened to the small creature repeat the words "Eee wah chu" over and over. When Bill returned home, he suddenly realized that the creature had been trying to speak English to him and what it was saying was, "We want you!" Could it have been a Pukwudgie?

• People who have encountered Pukwudgie feel confused and often find themselves wandering toward cliff edges.

Qiongqi
(*Chong Chee*)

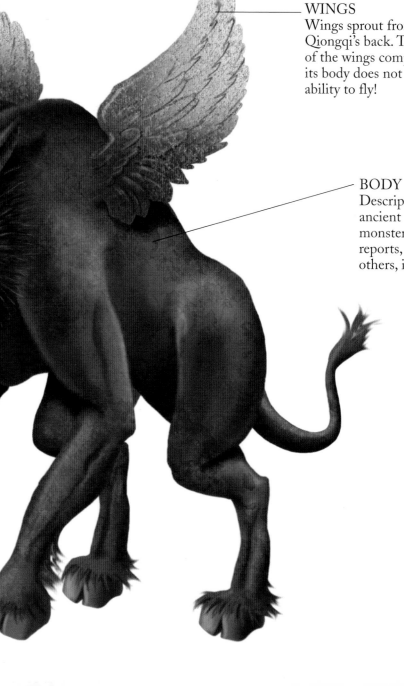

WINGS
Wings sprout from Qiongqi's back. The size of the wings compared to its body does not affect its ability to fly!

BODY
Descriptions of this ancient and deadly monster vary. In some reports, it is oxlike; in others, it is tigerlike.

MOUTH
Qiongqi feeds on humans whenever he can. However, he is also said to have a taste for evil spirits.

CRY
Qiongqi cries like a wild dog. The sound is enough to send a horrified chill through all those who hear it.

It is in one of Ancient China's most revered books—the *Shan Hai Jing* (*Classic of Mountains and Seas*)—that Qiongqi appears. The book dates from the 4th century BC and was compiled by many different authors over hundreds of years. The result is that Qiongqi is sometimes described as oxlike and sometimes tigerlike, with a foxtail and pair of large, feathered

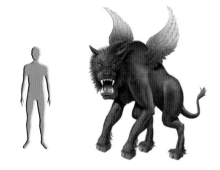

ACTUAL SIZE

wings. Qiongqi is a beast who revels in mischief, rewarding evil acts and punishing the virtuous. He does have one saving grace: Qiongqi's taste for evil is so great that he eats demon spirits, so his presence is often invoked to help drive them away.

▶ FU LING REGULARLY TRAVELED THE ROADS OF THE KINGDOM ALONE. Although he always carried his trusty sword, he used it more often to cut through the undergrowth than defend himself from bandits. Today, though, he was on his guard. He had been aware of being followed for some time and he'd timed his attack carefully. Pausing for a moment, as though to check his direction, he swung round, sword raised. However, nothing could have prepared him for the horror that lurked behind him…

Where in the world?

Like many Chinese legends, tales of Qiongqi were passed by word of mouth for generations before being written down. So they predate modern China by thousands of years!

●CHINA

Did you know?

● Qiongqi is referred to as one of four fiends who were banished by the Emperor Shun (2294–2184 BC) to the four corners of the empire. Although they are described as beasts, it is thought that these monsters were representations of four undesirable aspects of Chinese society and government.

● The four fiends were Qiongqi, Taowu, Taotie, and Hundun. Qiongqi represents deviousness. Some accounts say he is one of the Emperor Shaohao's sons (2600 BC), whose spirit has became resentful after death. Taowu is the beast of ignorance of learning and virtue. Taotie represents gluttony. He is often seen on ancient bronze food vessels and tableware. Hundun (see page 56) represents chaos, confusion, or stupidity. He may have been inspired by a lazy son of the Yellow Emperor (2698–2598 BC).

● The word "Qiongqi" is used to describe deceitful or treacherous people.

Red Ettin

(Red et-tin)

HEADS
In some tales, Ettins have just two heads, but the Red Ettin has three, making him even more unpleasant.

BRAINS
Ettins are usually described as violent and unintelligent, although the Red Ettin's love of puzzles suggests he is unusually cunning.

BODY
Big, broad, brawny, and fast on his feet, Red Ettin is built like an American pro-wrestling champion.

STOMACH
This giant has a giant appetite. Watch out that he doesn't grind up your bones to make his bread!

"Snouk butt and snouk ben, I find the smell of earthly man, He be living or he be dead, his heart this night will kitchen my bread."

The tale of Red Ettin has it all. Good fairies, captive princesses, a brave youth, and an evil giant who likes rhymes, riddles, and turning heroes into a late-night snack! Red Ettin is a three-headed Irish giant who kidnaps King Malcolm's daughter and keeps her as his slave. In the tale, retold in Andrew Lang's *Blue Fairy Book*, a young hero sets out to seek his fortune. On his journey he encounters an old woman, who begs him for a slice of bannock bread…

ACTUAL SIZE

▶ THE YOUTH HAD LITTLE TO EAT, but he gladly shared his food with the old woman. Later, as he approached the giant's castle, he was thankful that he had been so generous, for the old woman was a fairy in disguise. The giant, she said, would ask him three riddles and if he answered truly, then the Ettin's power would be broken forever. With the fairy's help, the hero solved the giant's riddles, took up his ax, and lopped off the monster's heads.

Where in the world?

Ettin is an Old English word for a giant. The Red (red-haired) Ettin of this tale is Irish, but the story itself comes from Scotland.

● SCOTLAND

Did you know?

. . . .

● The Ettin asks the hero three riddles. The first head asks: "What is a thing without an end?" To which the lad replies: "A globe." The second head asks: "The smaller the more dangerous; what's that?" To which the hero answers: "A bridge." The third and final head asks: "When does the dead carry the living?" The young man answers: "When a ship sails on the sea with men inside her."

● After he has killed the giant, the hero frees the Ettin's prisoners, including the king's daughter, who—in true fairy-tale tradition—he marries, and they live happily ever after.

● Scottish poet Andrew Lang published twelve books of fairy tales between 1889 and 1910. They are known as *Andrew Lang's Fairy Books of Many Colors*, as each book has a different colored cover. In all, Lang's series collected 437 tales.

Sandwalker

(Sand-wocker)

STINGER
The tip of the creature's tail carries a sharp stinger that is used to inject venom into its enemies and victims.

LEGS
Like real-life scorpions, the Sandwalker has eight legs, including a pair of oversized grasping claws (known as pedipalps).

TAIL
A narrow, segmented tail can be raised and curved up, over the Sandwalker's body, to strike at its victims in front.

SIZE
The Sandwalker is a huge beast—larger than a horse—and is easily able to carry away its victims.

In folk tales, all the really scary monsters come out at night—and the Sandwalker is no exception. By day, this giant hides away under the desert sands, but at night it comes out to hunt. Camels and horses are its snack of choice, but a creature of this size and power can pick and choose what—or who—its eats! The Sandwalker is a monster from Arabian myth that resembles a titanic scorpion, with crushing claws, the beak of an eagle, and a black carapace. Combined with its ability to walk silently and speedily across the shifting sands, this beast is one that is rightly feared by desert dwellers.

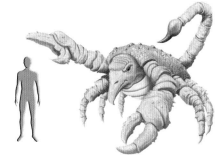

ACTUAL SIZE

▶ IT WAS DARK AMONG THE DUNES. Isra had been traveling all evening and the whistle of sand over the dunes was beginning to lull her to sleep. She was lucky. The horse had reared and thrown her to the ground before she had even registered the danger. Now, while the Sandwalker grappled with her mount, she had a chance to escape. She felt heartless leaving her terrified animal in the clutches of the devilish beast, but if she wanted to live, she would have no choice.

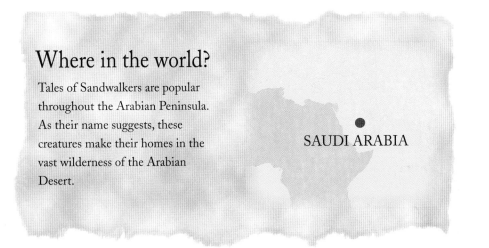

Where in the world?

Tales of Sandwalkers are popular throughout the Arabian Peninsula. As their name suggests, these creatures make their homes in the vast wilderness of the Arabian Desert.

● SAUDI ARABIA

Did you know?

● Sandwalkers appear in the 2012 fantasy film *Wrath of the Titans*.

● Arabia is home to many mythical monsters. The Roc, for instance, is a gigantic bird of prey, so large that it can carry off an elephant. The Dandan is the largest fish in the sea and is capable of swallowing a ship and her crew whole.

● Many of these beasts, spirits, and demons were popularized by stories that appear in *The Arabian Nights*. This is a collection of one thousand and one tales in which a bloodthirsty king kills off a succession of wives after their wedding night. His new wife, Scheherazade, saves herself by telling the king a story every evening, always leaving the tale unfinished so that he must let her live to complete the tale another night.

Sasabonsam

(Say-sa-bon-sam)

BODY
The Sasabonsam has a hairy, humanoid body and a bestial head. It is more batlike than Asanbosam, which has similar habits.

EYES
A pair of large, bloodshot eyes constantly scan the plains, on the lookout for easy pickings.

TEETH
This monstrous vampire is believed to have a set of iron teeth along with iron hooks on its feet.

WINGS
Some legends claim that Sasabonsam has a wingspan of about twenty feet (6.1 m). Its wings are leathery, like those of a bat.

Perched in the treetops, Sasabonsam is a horrifying sight. Although humanoid, this vampire has a beast's head and bat wings. In some accounts, it has a flaming mouth and a long tail that ends in the head of a snake, which coils around the tree in which it sits. Sasabonsam's favorite trick is to sit on a high branch and dangle its legs beneath, hoping to entangle any unwary traveler. Its feet, which are tipped with iron claws, point both ways, allowing the monster to grasp its victims from in front and behind. Its teeth, too, are made of iron, and are tough enough to tear into its prey's throat and spill its blood.

ACTUAL SIZE

▶ THE SUN WAS DAZZLINGLY BRIGHT and Yoofi had to squint to see the dusty tracks. Generations of his people had used the same routes, creating well-worn paths that criss-crossed the dry earth. Today, Yoofi was traveling to a distant village and, with the sun in his eyes, he couldn't tell if the track led right or straight ahead. He could see the shimmer of treetops ahead and finally decided to head toward the greenery. Perhaps he would even stop for a rest in the shade…

Where in the world?

These monsters come from the wonderful folklore of the Ashanti people of Southern Ghana, Ivory Coast, and Togo. They live and hunt in treetops.

● IVORY COAST

Did you know?

● Author J.K. Rowling, who wrote the *Harry Potter* series of books, mentions that Sasabonsams were used as mascots by the Nigerian National Quidditch Team during the 2014 Quidditch World Cup. According to an account in the wizarding newspaper, *The Daily Prophet*, the event was memorable for the level of injuries sustained even before the competition had begun.

● The Asanbosam is a similar creature to the Sasabonsam, only more human in appearance. Both vampires have iron teeth and hunt their victims from the treetops. Some scholars suggest that Asanbosam is an alternative name for Sasabonsam.

● The English explorer Sir Richard Burton wrote in his book *Wanderings in West Africa* that: "Sasabonsam is the friend of witch and wizard, hates priests and missionaries, and inhabits huge silk cotton trees in the gloomiest forests; he is a monstrous being of human shape."

Talos

(*Tah-loss*)

WINGS?
There are no written accounts of Talos ever having wings. However, some ancient Cretan coins show him as a winged giant.

BODY
Talos is made entirely of bronze. The poet Hesiod says he is the last survivor from the Age of Bronze (the third of humankind's five ages).

VEIN
A single vein runs from Talo's neck down to his ankle. Through this flows the bronze giant's lifeblood.

ANKLE
Like Achilles, who was invulnerable apart from a spot on his ankle, Talo's one weakness is a bronze nail in his ankle.

In Greek mythology, Talos makes his appearance in the adventures of Jason and the Argonauts when Jason's ship, the *Argo*, arrives in Crete. Talos, the last of the sons of the gods, is Crete's guardian. Three times a day, the bronze giant strides around the island, pulling down cliffs onto any ships that pass too close. His body is invulnerable, but one vein runs from his neck to his ankle, secured by a metal nail. When the *Argo's* crew are driven away, the sorceress Medea intervenes. Conjuring terrible visions in the giant's mind, Medea sends him into a frenzy in which he rips the nail out and his lifeblood runs away "like molten lead."

ACTUAL SIZE

▶ MEDEA THE SORCERESS stood on the deck of the ship, her arms raised towards the monstrous Talos. Raising her head defiantly, she began to sing—calling out to the spirits of death with a quiet, haunting melody. These swift phantoms feed on life and drive living creatures mad with terror. Talos gasped in horror as the hideous spirits whirled around his head—invisible to everyone except him.

Where in the world?

Crete is a Greek island in the Mediterranean Sea. Tales of Talos date from the Bronze Age (c. 1600–1100 BC), when Crete was part of Mycenaean civilization.

● CRETE

Did you know?

• In the well-known 1963 film version of *Jason and the Argonauts*, Jason is very much the hero of the tale. However, in the original epic poem, written by Apollonius of Rhodes, it is Medea whose knowledge and cunning help secure the magic Golden Fleece.

• Medea is the King of Colchis's daughter, who falls in love with Jason. The king agrees to give Jason the fleece if he fulfills three tasks. First, Jason has to plow a field with fire-breathing oxen. Medea provides him with a lotion to make him flame-proof. Second, he must sow a field with the teeth of the dragon. Medea warns him that the teeth will grow into skeletal warriors, and Jason escapes the trap. Finally, he has to overcome the dragon that guards the Fleece. Again, Medea comes to his aid with a potion that puts the guardian to sleep.

Tarbh Uisge

(*Tarv-ooshk*)

EARS
Tarbh Uisge has no ears.
If it mates with domestic
cattle, its offspring have
very small or split ears.

HORNS
Like real Highland
cattle, Tarbh Uisge
comes well equipped
for defense or attack,
with a pair of wicked-
looking horns.

CRY
Despite its impressive size,
Tarbh Uisge doesn't bellow
like an ordinary bull. Instead,
it crows like a cockerel.

BODY
A black, velvety pelt covers
the bull's muscular frame.
This helps camouflage it as
it emerges from the water
at night.

Tarbh Uisge is a water-bull from Scottish legend. At night, this bulky beast emerges out of lochs and coastal waters to feed and mate. Like the fierce Irish water-horse, Each Tened, this creature has the contrary nature of the fairy folk. At times, it can be placid and peaceful. At others, it is violent and deadly. According to the Reverend Dr. Alexander Stewart, writing in 1885, Tarbh Uisge has the same shape and form as the bull after which it is named, but Tarbh Uisge are "larger, fiercer, and with an amount of devilment and cunning about them."

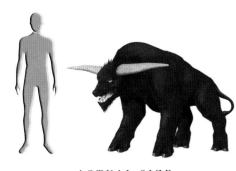

ACTUAL SIZE

▶ THE WATER-BULL ROARED DOWN THE LONELY LANE TOWARD THE WOMAN. However, Robina Ross hadn't lived her whole life in the Highlands without learning something of its legends and dangers. She always carried a gun and—just in case any trouble she found was of the more "unnatural" kind—a pocket of silver bullets. Her brother had laughed when she had melted down silver coins to make the pellets. But tonight, when she brought home the creature's carcass, there would be no more laughing.

Where in the world?

Tarbh Uisge lives in isolated lochs and coastal waters in the Highlands of Scotland. Loch Llundavra and Loch Achtriachtan in Glencoe are famous for water-bull legends.

● SCOTLAND

Did you know?

● Tarbh Uisge is Scottish Gaelic for water-bull. On the Isle of Man (an island off the coast of western England), the bull is known as Taroo Ustey. The phrase comes from the Manx language, which, like Scottish Gaelic, has Celtic roots.

● Some stories concerning these water sprites suggest that they can only be killed using silver bullets, like werewolves.

● The tale of Tarbh Uisge may have originated with the water spouts that can sometimes be seen on Scottish lochs. From a distance, these spouts may look like the figure of a bull or horse racing across the water's surface.

● In Manx legends, the offspring of Tarbh Uisge and ordinary cattle is a "rude lump of flesh and skin without bones." In the Highlands, the offspring are born healthy and are valued as bigger and stronger than normal cattle.

Tecumbalam

(Te-come-bal-am)

BILL
Instead of a mouth,
Tecumbalam has a
curved bill. This is
razor-sharp and is used
to rip and tear meat
from bone.

CLAWS AND TALONS
Equipped with the claws and
talons of a mighty bird of
prey, Tecumbalam can grip
his victim's flesh with ease.

WINGS
A pair of feathered wings allows
Tecumbalam to attack his prey
on the ground and at speed
without being heard.

BODY
This half-man, half-bird is
one of three bird-men from
Mayan myth. His brothers
are Xecotcovach, Camulatz,
and Cotzbalam.

It is the dawn of creation. There is no earth, only a calm sea and endless sky, wrapped in inky blackness. In this primal darkness the gods— the Creator, the Maker, Tepeu, Gucumatz, and the Forefathers—sit in solitude. Tepeu and Gucumatz decide that the emptiness and endless void should be filled. They form the earth, the mountains, and the valleys.

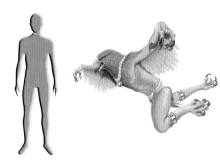

ACTUAL SIZE

They create animals, but they know that their creation will be worthless without man to praise it. So they fashion beings from wood, which, having neither soul nor intellect, angers the other gods. They dispatch the savage Tecumbalam and his bird-man brothers to do their bidding…

▶ "THE GODS, IRRITATED BY THEIR LACK OF REVERENCE, resolved to destroy the creations. By the will of Hurakan … the waters were swollen, and a great flood came upon the manikins of wood. They were drowned and a thick resin fell from heaven. The bird Xecotcovach tore out their eyes; the bird Camulatz cut off their heads; the bird Cotzbalam devoured their flesh; the bird Tecumbalam broke their bones and sinews and ground them into powder." (Translated from *The Popul Vuh* by Lewis Spence.)

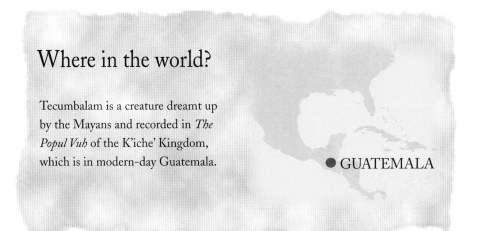

Where in the world?

Tecumbalam is a creature dreamt up by the Mayans and recorded in *The Popul Vuh* of the K'iche' Kingdom, which is in modern-day Guatemala.

● GUATEMALA

Did you know?

● Tecumbalam is a being from Mayan lore. He is mentioned in a book called *The Popul Vuh* (*Book of the People*), which is a record of native creation stories and legends.

● According to *The Popul Vuh*, the gods have made several attempts to create life. The first humans are made of earth and mud but dissolve. The second humans are created from wood. For the final and successful attempt, the gods made the flesh of humans from yellow and white corn and used cornmeal dough for their arms and legs. These "talked, conversed, saw and heard, walked, grasped things" and "were good and handsome men."

● Tecumbalam is the henchman—or rather henchbeast—of the bat god, Camazotz. The name "Camazotz" means "death bat," as he was associated with night, death, and ritual sacrifice.

Tugarin Zmeyevich

(Tu–ga–rin Zmee–vitch)

WINGS
These massive wings may look impressive, but they have a fatal flaw. They are made of nothing but thin paper!

MOUTH
From this terrible lizard's mouth comes fire, smoke, and red-hot sparks. Tugarin also throws burning logs at his opponents.

SKIN
The dragon's skin is covered in tough scales that act just like armor to protect Tugarin Zmeyevich during battles.

BODY
Tugarin is a monstrous dragon with an eel-like body. In some accounts, his torso is covered in fiery, writhing snakes.

Almost every nation has a tale of a brave knight who risks life and limb to fight a fire-breathing dragon. In a Slavic story of heroism and guile, the hero, Alyosha Popovich, challenges the dragon Tugarin Zmeyevich to a duel after the monster insults the king at a banquet. Tugarin is a cruel and savage dragon, with the power to throw fire, smoke, and red-hot tree trunks at his enemies. Despite his enormous size, he is a creature of magic and can fly, supported by a pair of paper wings. When Alyosha arrives for the battle, Tugarin is already airborne and poised to rain down a fury of fire and brimstone on our hero...

ACTUAL SIZE

▶ ALYOSHA POPOVICH STARED AT THE DRAGON WITH SICKLY DREAD. The sight of the creature hovering in the air above him was horrifying. He knew that he would never beat the beast in an honest fight. He needed to be clever! He had noticed earlier that the dragon's wings were made of paper, so, closing his eyes for a moment, he offered up a silent prayer. If only God would grant him some rain, then the beast's paper wings would literally become his downfall.

Where in the world?

This beast comes from stories told by the Kievan Rus—a federation of Eastern Slavic tribes—who inhabited Belarus, the Ukraine, and Russia.

● BELARUS   ●RUSSIA
● UKRAINE

Did you know?

● At the end of the tale, God sends a rainstorm and Tugarin's paper wings are ruined by the water. The dragon plummets to the ground, allowing Alyosha to close in and kill the beast.

● Tales of Alyosha Popovich were first told in *bylinas*. These are a type of tale that has been passed on by word of mouth. In such stories, Alyosha is famous for his tricks and humor.

● Alyosha Popovich is a *bogatyr*, which is a Slavic word for a hero or knight. The three most popular *bogatyrs* are Alyosha Popovich, Dobrynya Nokotich, and Ilya Muromets. Each of these heroes has his own traits. Alyosha is cunning; Dobrynya is brave, and Ilya is the more spiritual of the trio.

● Scholars say that Alyosha Popovich represents Christian, Eastern Slavic Europe. Tugarin Zmeyevich represents pagan superstition and magic.

Tupilaq

(*Too-pi-lak*)

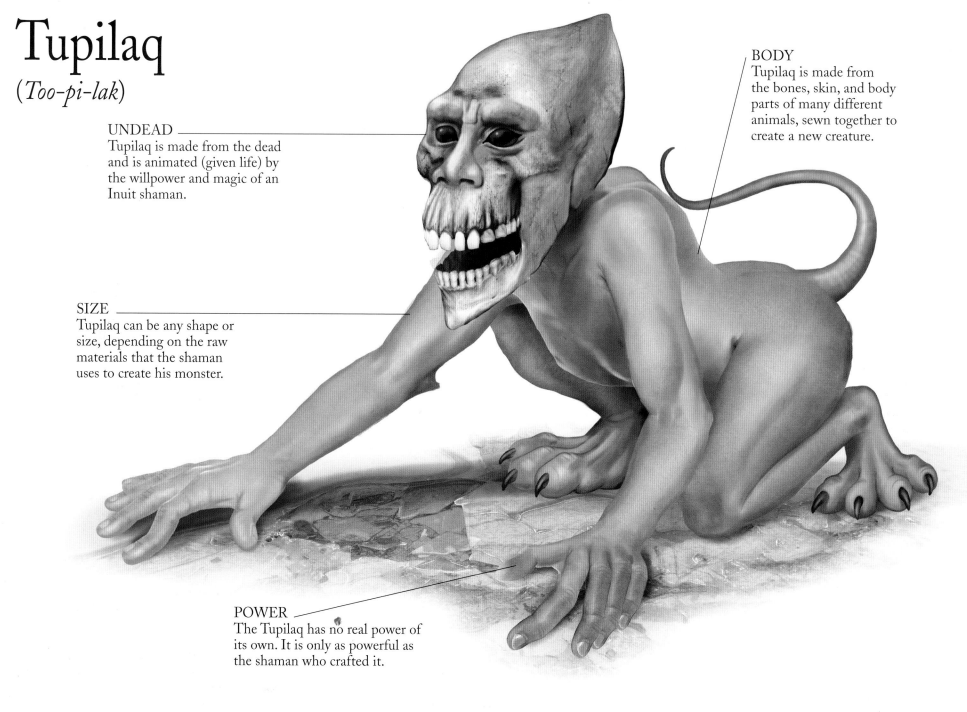

UNDEAD
Tupilaq is made from the dead and is animated (given life) by the willpower and magic of an Inuit shaman.

SIZE
Tupilaq can be any shape or size, depending on the raw materials that the shaman uses to create his monster.

POWER
The Tupilaq has no real power of its own. It is only as powerful as the shaman who crafted it.

BODY
Tupilaq is made from the bones, skin, and body parts of many different animals, sewn together to create a new creature.

From Inuit myth, the Tupilaq is an undead monster made from the body parts of animals and children, sewn together and animated by witchcraft. Taking many days to create, the Shaman works on his abominable creation in secret, even wearing his anorak backward so that the Tupilaq won't know his identity. Finally, as his chants and rituals work their magic, Tupilaq stirs and begins to look for a victim. However, such foul magic can have dangerous side effects. Should the shaman's enemy be more powerful than him, then he runs the risk of Tupilaq being turned against him.

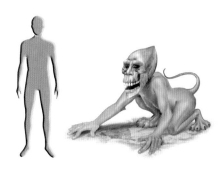

ACTUAL SIZE

▶ KEELUT KNELT FACING THE BEAST. Although his face was covered by his anorak, he could still hear the creature's ragged breathing and the scratching of its long fingers as it scrabbled at the earth. The Tupilaq was newly made. It was still learning how to use its misshapen body, and the unearthly sounds it made sent Keelut's stomach lurching. Soon, though, it would be ready to do his bidding. It would be ready to leave the hut and destroy those who had opposed him.

Where in the world?

The Tupilaq is a beast from the tales of Greenland's Inuit peoples. Similar beings exist in Canadian Inuit myths, although they are spirits, not physical creations.

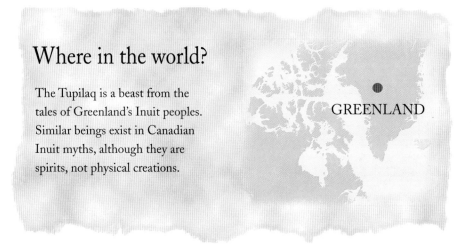

GREENLAND

Did you know?

● In Canadian Inuit traditions, the Tupilaq is a ghost or destructive spirit. It can only be seen and driven away by a shaman.

● Inuit craftspeople carved images of the Tupilaq in whalebone to show explorers what the creatures looked like. These miniature sculptures are now highly collectable.

● Western culture often regards shamans as a type of witch or sorcerer. In reality, the shaman is more like the community scholar. He has special knowledge and abilities—especially of the spirit world—and uses these things to help his people.

● During rituals, the shaman may speak to those in the spirit world. However, he must avoid referring to people or objects by their ordinary names as this will bring bad luck to those people or objects. Some shamans therefore have their own spirit language. This is rich in poetry and symbolism.

Index